THE PURSUIT OF LEGENDARY FATHERHOOD

Copyright © 2025 Larry Hagner

All rights reserved. No part of this publication may be reproduced, distributed, or transmitted in any form or by any means, including photocopying, recording, digital scanning, or other electronic or mechanical methods, without the prior written permission of the author, except in the case of brief quotations embodied in critical reviews and certain other noncommercial uses permitted by copyright law.

ISBN: 979-8-218-69284-1

Printed in the USA

CONTENTS

Introduction. 1

Part 1: Let's Set the Stage 5
   Chapter 1: The First Father I Remember 7
   Chapter 2: The Beginning of the Drift. 11
   Chapter 3: The Drift. 21
   Chapter 4: The Five Dimensions of Manhood/Fatherhood/
      Husbandhood. 29

Part 2: Husband. 45
   Chapter 5: Creating an Extraordinary Marriage. 47
   Chapter 6: The Secret No One Tells You About Marriage 51
   Chapter 7: The 4 Elements of an Extraordinary Marriage 54
   Chapter 8: Date Her. 96
   Chapter 9: Listen for Feelings, Not Just Words 100
   Chapter 10: The Quality of Your Relationship Is Determined
      by the Quality of Your . . . Questions 105
   Chapter 11: It's a WE, Not You or Me 110
   Chapter 12: Lead Her 113
   Chapter 13: Never Be Afraid to Ask for What You Want,
      Need, or Desire. 118

Part 3: Father. 123
   Chapter 14: Connection with Kids 125

Chapter 15: Skill #1 – Love Your Wife in Front of Your Kids. . 127
Chapter 16: Skill #2 – Patience Is a SKILL, Not a FEELING...
   So Learn the Skill. 131
Chapter 17: Skill 3 – Kids Spell "L-O-V-E," "T-I-M-E" 152
Chapter 18: Skill #4 – Create an Environment of Psychological
   Safety So Your Kids Will Come to You with Everything . . . 155
Chapter 19: Raising Young Men 166
Chapter 20: Raising Young Women 195

Part 4: Leader. 217
   Chapter 21: Lead YOURSELF First!. 219
   Chapter 22: Rules for Leadership 222

Conclusion 267
Exercise: Identifying Your Core Values 268
Letter to Mason. 276

INTRODUCTION

"The Definition of Hell is being on your deathbed and meeting the man you could have become."
– Author Unknown

Before you dive into the following chapters of this book, it's important that you start right here!

Go back and read that quote above one more time. How does it feel? Does it hit you right in the heart? Does it give you the chills? Does it scare you? Does it motivate the hell out of you to become more? Do you suddenly feel a sense of urgency to get into your life and live your best life versus drifting?

If the answer is "YES," then keep reading because this is your life. We have one shot at it. We literally have one go at this whole thing! Not only do we only have one shot to live a legendary life, but most of us are not even living close to what we truly want!

In fact, the majority of us are walking the planet right now in "the drift." We are simply drifting through life and not living with everything we have.

Maybe you don't have the marriage you hoped you would. It might be the lack of communication. Maybe it's the lack of intimacy. Perhaps it's having little to no sex and passion. It could be that you no longer feel there is a spark, a fire, and a purpose. It doesn't matter what it is; all you know is it's not what you intended for your marriage or even what you envisioned. As a result, you drift.

Maybe you are drifting in your journey with your kids. You might be raising a brand-new baby and you have no clue what you are doing. All you know is that you are overwhelmed and simply surviving one sleepless night to the next. As a result, you drift.

Perhaps you are raising your kids through the toddler phase, and you have no clue how to interact and play with them. You have no idea how to connect with this little person. So, you drift.

Your kids might be in their teenage years right now, and you're wondering why they won't talk to you. Maybe they're in a season, long or short, where they respond with only one word or two, leaving you frustrated and wondering what could be wrong. So, you drift.

Maybe your own physical, mental, emotional, and spiritual health have taken a backseat since you married and became a father. After all, how are you supposed to take care of you? You have to take care of everyone else, right? As a result, you've neglected yourself. You don't feel as mentally clear. Your emotions are up and down. Perhaps you just bury any emotion that makes you uncomfortable (like most men do). Instead of dealing with emotions like sadness, anger, depression, or even isolation, you simply self-medicate with vices. As your stress, anger, resentment, or sadness elevates, you dive deeper into habits that numb the pain (porn, alcohol, drugs, etc.).

If you have read this far because you can relate to any or all of the above, then buckle your seatbelt for the rest of this book.

I have lived every single one of these scenarios and more. This book is meant to help you identify where you are in your journey as a man, husband, and father. It's also going to give you simple and effective ways to disrupt the drift and take back control of your life, marriage, career/business, health (physical, mental, emotional, and spiritual), parenting journey, and even finances.

Gentlemen, this book is written straight from my heart. Some of it (if not all of it) will be a kick in the rear, a shot between the eyes, and it will force you to give yourself a good hard look in the mirror to identify where you are in your life and what you can do about it.

This book has several different stories, topics, and strategies to help you LIVE LEGENDARY (you will read those two words a lot in the upcoming pages).

If you are sick and tired of not having the life you have always envisioned and are ready to take meaningful action that truly counts and truly matters, then LET'S GO!!

Let's stop drifting and start living.

PART 1

LET'S SET THE STAGE

1 THE FIRST FATHER I REMEMBER

"My father gave me the greatest gift anyone could ever give another person: He believed in me."

— Jim Valvano

On February 12, 2012, I saw the look of absolute fear and terror in my four-year-old son's eyes as I went to help him up off the ground after I had spanked him in a fit of rage.

At this time in my life, I had been married for nine years. I had two boys (five and four years old). At the age of 12, I had sworn to myself that I would never strike my child in anger. I knew the feeling of being terrified by my father all too well.

Backing up for a moment to share some context. My mom and biological father were married in 1971. I was born in 1975. When I was about nine months old, my parents separated and got divorced. My father simply vanished out of my young life and started a new life for himself. I have no recollection of my biological father; no memories of any type of interaction with him. It was almost like he never existed.

My first introduction to the concept of a "father" was when I was in preschool, at the young age of four. Before that, I had no frame of reference. I remember being seeing men (fathers) pick up my friends at preschool, so I was able to piece together what a father was. I knew that most of my friends and even extended family members had them, but I didn't. This didn't bother me at all. I didn't feel like I was missing out. In fact, my understanding of a father at this point in my life was that moms go out and find dads. In my mind, dads were never a part of the beginning equation. They simply entered into the family once the mom found them and brought them into the family. My understanding of me not having a dad in my life boiled down to the simple fact that my mom had not found my dad yet. I was hopeful. He was out there somewhere. I was OK with waiting, and I didn't feel like I was missing a thing. At this point in my life, my mom was affectionate. We got along well. She loved me and she showed it. I never felt deprived.

Up until this point, the only father figure in my life was my grandfather. I never had a man to guide me, raise me, hug me, tuck me in at night, or read me a bedtime story. Again, it didn't bother me. I knew no different.

I will never forget the first time a man entered my home and life at the tender, vulnerable age of four. I remember that day like it was yesterday. My mom had been dating a man for a few weeks she met at work. She decided to ask him over for dinner and to meet me. As I patiently awaited his arrival, I was nervous. I remember that I constantly went to the window to see if he was there yet. My heart was beating fast. Even my hands were sweaty. *Could this actually be the moment I had been waiting for? Was the man that I was about to meet going to be my new father? After all, this could be the man my mom found to be my dad.* As I waited, thoughts of what our family would look like if it were complete raced through my mind. I started thinking about family dinners with the three of us sitting at the table, talking about our day, laughing, and telling stories. I thought about what it would be like if I had a dad who would play soccer with me out in the backyard or even take me fishing. I thought about what it would be like for a for a dad to put me to bed at night and read me my favorite *Curious George* bedtime story. The more I thought about all these visions and images, the more nervous I got.

My thoughts were interrupted by a knock at the door. I knew who it was. Suddenly, I was even more nervous but also extremely excited to meet this man who was going to become my dad—he just didn't know it at the time.

My mom walked to the door with excitement. They had only been dating for a few weeks, so no doubt she was in the honeymoon phase of their courtship. She opened the door, and they greeted each other with a warm smile and an embrace. To date, I had never seen my mom hug or kiss a man besides my grandfather. Seeing this for the first time was surreal.

He wore a three-piece suit with pinstripes. In the middle of the suit, starting at the bottom of his neck, was a maroon double Windsor tie. Covering the suit was a light brown trench coat, and he carried a briefcase in his right hand. There were no iPads or laptops in 1979, so a white-collared software engineer had to carry all of his documents and paperwork in a briefcase. No doubt a symbol of status, and the way he dressed emulated his high ranks in the computer company he worked for at the time.

I was intimidated at first. This man was so much taller and bigger than me. I could smell his Old Spice cologne as he entered our house. Definitely a masculine scent that I had never smelled under my own roof to date.

After their warm embrace, my mom turned to look at me with a warm, welcoming look on her face, encouraging me to come over and meet this man. She reached out her hand and invited me to take four steps forward to shake hands.

"Larry, this is Joe," she said.

I was now toe to toe with the giant well-dressed man. He looked down at me and smiled warmly. I could see the happiness in his smile as his handlebar mustache raised. He extended his hand to shake mine. I don't remember a handshake with anyone before this man, but somehow, I still knew what to do.

He embraced my hand firmly, and with a gentle yet low, masculine voice he said, "Nice to meet you, Larry. I have heard so many good things about you."

As I held his hand and looked up at him with awe, words came bursting out of my mouth without any thought or control. I smiled from ear to ear with excitement. The words flowed. I couldn't control them. They just came out.

"Are you going to be my dad?" I asked with excitement, joy, and nervousness.

The environment suddenly changed. I remember seeing the look of absolute disbelief on his face. His warm smiling face went to absolute shock and awe. He and my mom looked at each other speechless.

"One thing at a time, young man. One thing at a time," he said warmly.

It was in that moment I knew my life would change. In that moment, I had nothing but good feelings that our family would soon be complete.

2 THE BEGINNING OF THE DRIFT

> *"Some people drift through their entire life. They do it one day at a time, one week at a time, one month at a time. It happens so gradually they are unaware of how their lives are slipping away until it's too late."*
>
> — Mary Kay Ash

After only about a year of my mom and Joe dating, their wedding day arrived! Perhaps my crazy awkward question was the catalyst to a thought process that propelled their relationship to the next level. To this day I don't know if that was the case or if it was fate that my mom and Joe would be married.

At any rate, I was so happy and excited to have a man/father in my life that would show me love and affection. I was eager to learn about sports and work with my hands, side by side with my dad, as I grew up. Joe had become my hero, and he didn't even know it. Not only did he not know it; he hadn't even earned the right to be my hero.

THE PURSUIT OF LEGENDARY FATHERHOOD

If there is one thing I have learned working with men, fathers, and husbands over the past 10 years, it is that we are our kids' heroes. Often, we don't realize it because we simply do not see ourselves through our children's eyes. In most cases, we haven't even earned the title of hero through our actions. Think about that for a moment and really let that sink in. As you read these words right now, YOU ARE YOUR KID'S HERO. Like it or not, you have that title, and maybe you don't think you've earned it. He or she looks up to you as their guide, role model, and foundation. Most likely we will go our entire lives as fathers and never come close to loving ourselves or holding ourselves up in such a high regard as our kids do! You might not think of yourself as a hero or even close to that, but your kids do! Take 60 seconds and ponder that before you read on because it is absolutely true.

As most marriages begin, my mom and Joe's marriage started with the best of intentions. Looking back on the time they were married (six years), I honestly don't know if my mom truly loved him or if she desperately wanted a companion for her and a dad for me.

Before Joe came along, my mom worked long hours to support us. I saw her in the evenings and weekends. I was in daycare throughout the week. She absolutely did what she had to do to provide for us. She worked hard, and looking back, I could tell we were financially strapped and things were tight. We got quick fast food here and there and for entertainment, my mom would take me to an airport parking lot where we would watch the airplanes fly over. It was awesome how creative she got with ideas for free entertainment.

The first year of marriage to Joe seemed like a breath of fresh air. My mom was able to quit her full-time job, which meant I no longer had to go to childcare after school. She was able to pick me up every day. She was home every day. She made dinners for us, and there was hardly any fast food or eating on the run. Everything at home seemed like it was settling down. My mom didn't seem as lonely or even stressed. My mom was able to get a new car. Holidays and birthdays were more extravagant with an increase in income. Joe ended up legally adopting me shortly after they got married, but I don't remember calling him anything other than "Dad" before then. He was "Dad" right from the start.

As their marriage progressed over the next five years, I began to notice a change in their relationship and a change with each of them individually.

Over time, I noticed stress between the two of them was higher. They weren't as affectionate with each other. Slowly yet suddenly, I saw their relationship begin to drift. What started with the best of intentions ended with five years of hell between them, and I was deeply involved.

When I saw my dad lose the light in his eyes—that signified the beginning of the drift.

I was interviewing a guest on *The Dad Edge Podcast*, and I will never forget one question he asked me:" Do you remember the day when you saw your dad lose the light in his eyes?"

That question hit me like a punch in the chest. Not only do I relate to that question, but I have no doubt as you reflect on this question right now, you will most likely remember that moment as well. Many of us who are fathers right now were raised differently. Too many fathers that raised our generation were providers. They were a part of our lives and maybe even played some critical roles, but they weren't IN our lives. Too many of us raising kids in this current day and age were raised by men who raised us at an arm's length. "MAN UP!" "TOUGHEN UP!" "BABIES CRY! MEN DON'T!" Now, don't get me wrong, there is a time and place for tough love and definitely boundaries so we aren't raising a generation of wet sponges who cave at the first sign of adversity. However, too many of the dads who raised us had very low levels of emotional intelligence. To add insult to injury, there were virtually zero resources for men who wanted to step up their game as dads and husbands. They only knew what they knew, and to be bluntly honest, they did the best they could with what they had—just as we are!

I remember when my dad lost the light in his eyes. December 25, 1980 was a night I will never forget. The evening ended in the 3:00 a.m. hour with blood on my mother's hands and on my dad's face with a police officer between the two of them.

We had spent the entire evening at my grandparents' celebrating Christmas Eve. It was a typical Christmas Eve that I was used to, even at such a young age. The evening started with five o' clock mass, followed by an elaborate turkey dinner made by my grandmother. After dinner, we all sat in a circle, opening up what Santa had brought us during five o' clock mass. My grandmother always had this amazing story that Santa would visit certain homes when he knew families were out at church so he didn't have to come back later that night, being that he was so busy making his trip around the world.

The evening seemed perfect as I opened up presents and new Star Wars toys. My mom and dad had smiles on their faces the whole time as they kicked back their drinks for the evening. My mom drinking her wine and my dad drinking Busch beer. I have no idea how many drinks were had, but I do know it lasted the whole night.

It was early into the morning hours of Christmas Day (around 2:00 a.m.) when we packed up the car with all of our gifts. There was tension in the air between my dad and mom. They were barely speaking to each other, and when they did, there were short, tense answers with only one or two words. I couldn't tell what the tension or problem was between the two of them, but it was apparent because I could feel it through the air. The tension was so thick, you could cut it with a knife.

My father was driving, and my mom was in the passenger seat. I was sitting in the backseat of their beautiful 1970 yellow Camaro with a sporty black pinstripe down the side (my mom's dream car). They started to argue about how much my dad drank when we pulled out of the driveway and began the one-mile trip back to our house. The yelling got louder as the car pulled out of the driveway and onto the road. Suddenly, with no warning, my dad floored the gas. I heard the Camaro's V8 engine roar. I engine hit a decibel that I didn't think was possible and certainly had never heard before. I don't know how fast we were going, and I didn't care because I wasn't focused on the speedometer. The only thing that was in my sights was the giant concrete pole with a massive streetlight on top that illuminated the dark street.

As we came closer to the pole, I screamed in absolute terror. I had never been in a car accident, and this was going to be my first. I heard my mom scream, "JOE, STOP THE CAR!!!" It was a scream that I had never heard before that day. It was a scream of anger and absolute terror. It filled the interior of that car, and God knows who else heard it. Suddenly, I was thrust forward, hitting the front seats face first. My sight went black as I was met with the smell of leather from the seat in front of me. The car stood at a halt in the middle of the empty street. I put my hands on my nose as I felt something run from my nose and into my mouth. I instinctively put my hands on my nose because of the pressure and pain. As I looked at my hands, my fingers and palms were covered in blood. The force of my now-bleeding face hitting the seat sent a shockwave through it. I looked up at my parents in front of me, and the volume of screaming and yelling coming from my mom was deafening. She was slapping and beating my father. I had no clue what to do. This was the first time I'd ever seen my mother strike him. My father didn't hit back, but he did restrain her. My mom was screaming, crying, and yelling with anger. After what seemed like an eternity, she calmed down enough for my dad to let her go.

She demanded that she drive. My father wasn't having it. He told her to shut up and sit still as he put the car back in drive and we restarted the one-mile drive back home. The car was swerving as he tried to gain composure. My mom continued to yell at him to stay in his lane.

It was at this point when I began to panic. I held pressure on my nose, still bleeding. As my eyes filled up with tears of pain from my nose and fear from the tension in the car, I could see a blood spot where my face hit the white leather on the back of the front passenger seat.

I was terrified. What usually only took two minutes to drive from my grandparents' back home seemed like hours. I began to cry. I wasn't crying quietly. I was sobbing.

"Larry! SHUT UP! Stop being a damn baby! Stop crying!! STOPPPP CRYING NOW!!!" Joe yelled with rage.

The more he yelled, the more I cried. The bark in his deep voice was terrifying and ear piercing.

My mom came to my defense. "STOP YELLING AT HIM! HE IS SCARED!"

"SHUT UP! He is being a baby!" he barked back at my mom.

The car took a sudden and fast right turn into our driveway. It wasn't the normal speed one would pull into the driveway—more like the normal speed if you were going to drive right through the garage door and into the kitchen.

The car came to a sudden halt, and my dad violently put the car in park. I was still crying, even harder now. I was terrified by the way he was driving, the yelling, the blood on the seat in front of me and in my hands.

The driver-side door opened swiftly. Without even taking the time to close his door, my dad folded the driver-side seat in half and grabbed me violently with both hands by my shirt. As I began to cry louder with fear, my dad's hands climbed from gripping my shirt to my throat. His hands were cold from the brisk air. His breath reeked of alcohol. His eyes puffy, red, and filled with rage. He began to strangle my throat. The airway from my mouth to my chest no longer felt connected. I tried to scream, but nothing would come out. Suddenly, his rage intensified as he began to shake me back and forth. His face was within inches of mine. His teeth were grinding as he kept telling me to shut up over and over and over.

Suddenly, he let go and fell to the ground. I didn't know what happened, but he was doubled over, holding his face. My mom was standing over him, holding her 1979 dense wooden purse. I have no clue why wooden purses were a fashion statement back in the 1970s, but that night, that fashion statement might have saved my life.

My dad uncovered his face, but I couldn't make out where he was struck or if there was any damage done. All I knew is that he let me go. The next thing I knew, my mom was running towards the house. I have no doubt she was trying to get away from the madman she had just struck and had no clue what was going to happen next. At any rate, her fight-or-flight response went from fight to flight. My dad gained his composure and staggered to the front door after her. He began yelling, and threats of what he was going to do to her were now loud enough for our entire street to hear.

I have no clue what bravery came over me or why I thought a 40-pound me could stop a 200-plus, five-foot-eleven, full-grown man, but at any rate, I grabbed him by the right leg and held on for dear life. Looking back on it, I think my motive was to outmuscle him like all the *Incredible Hulk* shows I had seen on TV with Lou Ferrigno. My anger had taken over, which made me feel invincible. The protector in my five-year-old being came thrusting out in me.

I was quickly reminded how outmatched I really was as I was picked up once again by the throat with cold hands. This felt much stronger and more forceful than the first grasp. I had zero control as I was held by the throat and lifted off the ground. I again tried to scream, but nothing came out. The only thing I could do was kick my legs. I kicked them as hard and as fast as I could, landing one after another against him. I could tell it was working because his grip loosened. Suddenly, I was dropped once again. This time, I saw what happened before I was dropped.

Seeing me getting lifted in the air once again sent my mom into mama-bear mode. The wooden-purse weapon met the right side of my dad's face and sent him to the ground. I will never forget the sound of that wooden purse meeting human flesh and bone—a sound like hitting a solid wall. Then, a gasp of air that exited my dad's mouth as the strike sent him plummeting towards the earth in our front yard. I got up. I ran to my mom, who put her arm around me and quickly led me inside. My mom shut and locked the door. I went to the window to see make sure we were no longer in harm's way and that the monster that was my dad that night was no longer coming after us.

I saw him get to his feet as his hands covered his face in pain. I knew he was hurt and hurt badly. He stumbled towards the door.

He looked like a professional fighter who had a lights-out strike to the chin and was trying to stumble his way back to the center of the ring. He slowly stumbled towards the door, where he tried to turn the knob that was now securely locked.

"Debbie!! Let me in!" he demanded in a low, drunken tone.

"Let me in or I will break down the damn door!" he began to yell.

What was most likely 60 seconds of him yelling and banging on the door felt like an absolute eternity. I started to panic, wondering what would happen if he broke down the door. *Would he beat us? Kill us? Would he shoot us?* I knew he had a gun in the house, but I didn't know where it was. *Would this be the end of my life?*

Suddenly, I heard roaring engines in the distance. Red and blue lights bounced off the dark street and homes. The sounds of police sirens filled the quiet Christmas Eve night. I knew this wasn't Santa Claus coming to town. Three police were flying down the street and towards my house. One was coming from one side of my house and the other two from the other side. The one on the right side flew into our driveway, and the other two parked right in front of our home on the street. Three officers exited their cars simultaneously and carefully made their way towards the drunk, bleeding monster that was standing at our front door.

"Sir, don't move!" one of them shouted. No guns were drawn, but they were all on the ready.

My dad, no longer fighting, started explaining, "My wife hit me in the face twice with her wooden purse! I'm hurt badly and I think my nose is broken!"

"Sir, calm down!" one of the officers demanded.

With a calm voice, my dad agreed.

My heart was racing. *What will happen now? Will my dad go to jail? Will it just be me and my mom again? Have I lost my dad for life?*

The answer to the final question, "Have I lost my dad for life?", was "Yes and no."

That was the night I saw the sparkle in my father's eye disappear. For the next six years, he wasn't the same man. That night began his journey of his drift. He never really fully showed up in my life after that night. He traveled for work Monday through Friday for the next several years, and I only saw him on the weekends. Even when he was home on the weekends, he wasn't really there. He spent a lot of time in our basement, in the garage, or doing yard work. Anything to keep him from being a dad or husband with a purpose. He provided financially, but I could tell the marriage was only surface level between my mom and him. He simply physically existed in our home on the weekends. Any and all interactions had very little depth. He was gone.

3 THE DRIFT

> *"It is most appalling to know that 95% of the people of the world are drifting aimlessly through life, without the slightest conception of the work for which they are best fitted, and with no conception whatsoever of even the need of such a thing as a definite objective toward which to strive."*
>
> — Napoleon Hill

You will hear me reference "the drift" several times in this book. So, what is the drift? How does the drift impact us as men, husbands, and fathers? How does it even happen? How do we recognize and stop it? What happens to our lives, relationships, marriages, and businesses if we do not interrupt the drift?

For many men, this world becomes our reality. The drift is a real thing. The drift can even happen without us knowing. In fact, it can be the biggest and sneakiest bamboozle that we can experience in our lives.

Most men have a deep desire to show up big and intentionally in their lives, marriages, and for their kids, only to go to their grave regretting they didn't give it everything they had. We get wrapped up in work, surface-level friendships, feeling trapped in a job we hate, feeling helpless that we don't know how to create the connection with our wives we truly want, and not making time to make connections and the memories with our kids we truly want.

So, we subtly check out. It usually doesn't happen in a drastic way. It's usually never an overwhelming, catastrophic event that we can remember. It just slides in under the radar. We wake up and realize that we are living a life we never really set out to live. We spent hours upon hours working in jobs we despise. We never really chased our dreams or purpose in our lives. We settled for mediocrity in our jobs, marriages, health, and relationships with our kids. We have friendships with little to no depth. Most of our conversations with other men can be answered with three words: "Good," "Fine," or "Busy." All which are four-letter words!

A friend asks, "How's life?"

We answer, "Good!"

"How's work?"

"Busy!"

"How's the family?"

"Fine!"

It doesn't really matter which question is asked because any one of these can be answered with one of the four-letter words. We just decide which one at the time.

The drift will also impact our physical, mental, and emotional health. Men by nature are noble beings. At the end of the day, we desire to serve and provide. When it comes to our own physical, mental, and emotional health, we are the first to let those die on the sword with the perception we are doing it to serve others. We might even feel guilty or that it's selfish to take care of ourselves because that's what society tells us.

So, we become unhealthier as years pass by. We gain more weight and have less energy. We have even coined the term "the dad bod" as a way to excuse us from optimizing our physical health. We settle for it. In fact, we expect it to happen. But our physical, mental, and emotional health doesn't have to take a backseat. It can be a foundational tool that allows us to have more energy for our kids, more productivity in the workplace, and more connections in our relationships.

The drift will also impact our marriages. Think about couples you know that settle for a marriage that is disconnected; they do nothing about it because they think that being disconnected is something that is inevitable with all marriages. When we allow our marriages to go on autopilot and neglect intimacy, connection, optimal communication, and even the friendship we have with our spouse, it's like a slow death to our relationship. When we simply start existing under the same roof, binge watching Netflix, or simply sitting next to each other while we separately scroll through the never-ending BS of social media, we are burning up precious time that we could be using to connect with our soulmate. No one ever went to their grave saying: "I'm so glad we spent so many hours binge watching *Ozark* and didn't connect with each other!"

The drift will also impact our finances. Most of us aren't intentional when it comes to our family finances. Most of us don't know how to manage money. In reality, the majority of adults today have never been taught and have never taken a personal finance course. Many of us are drowning in debt and losing sleep at night, wondering how we are going to pay the next credit card bill or mortgage payment. But we simply continue to drift, put our heads in the sand, and build higher amounts of debt that is accompanied by stress. Every moment we spend stressing over our finances is another moment we aren't focusing on other things like optimal health, elevated relationships, and growth.

Finally, the drift will impact the relationships we have with our kids. There is no manual, no training, and no playbook for parenting. When we are left to "figure it out," it's easy to "check out." We can be physically present with our kids, but many of us do not have the physical, mental, and emotional connection with our kids that we truly desire. As a result, we wing it. When we wing it, we don't truly enjoy and embrace the journey. When we wing it, we also tend to make mistakes and not learn from them. We don't learn new skills to connect with our kids and build the solid foundation we truly want.

When we don't have the knowledge, skills, or even mentors in our life to help guide us through our drift, it will impact our confidence and fulfillment. When our confidence is impacted, it tremendously impacts how we show up in our lives. When we don't feel confident, we tend to feel unworthy or even shame. The feelings of guilt, shame, or unworthiness are like a cancer that sets in and impacts all that should be positive in our lives. These feelings can literally hinder everything and every relationship in our lives. To add insult to injury, when we allow these feelings to rule our minds and these perspectives go unchecked, it's simply easier to keep living within the drift of unhappiness because the very thought of our existence and relationships being positive are immediately halted by the feeling of being unworthy.

Unfortunately, most men are drifting to some degree in one or several areas of their lives. We might be thriving in our careers. We might make a ton of money and maybe even have the title we have always wanted on our LinkedIn profile, but our home life might be an absolute wreck. Most men would agree that a successful career and deep pockets are nice things to have, but not at the expense of living with strangers under your own roof.

Maybe we married the person of our dreams and have a strong marriage, but are drifting in our family finances. If our finances are not in order, the relationship and even the entire family unit can be built on a house of cards. Everyone knows that the divorce rate in the US is 50 percent. What you may not know is that 50 percent of those divorces are due to financial distress, money arguments, or the couple feeling absolutely crippled under a mountain of debt.

We could be thriving in our parenting journey as a father. Maybe you are one of those men who doesn't struggle with patience and genuinely enjoy doing everything you possibly can for your kids. In fact, you and your wife might be on the same page with this one. Perhaps when it comes to your family dynamics, everything is about the kids, and your marriage is the dimension that takes the backseat. This is really common. While always putting the kids first at every turn feels like the right thing to do, you start to notice a significant disconnect with your wife. Many married couples put so much attention on being parents that they forget about being a connected married couple. While this feels like the right thing to do, I highly encourage you to rethink this perspective. One of the greatest lessons we can teach our kids is how to create an extraordinary marriage. Many married couples feel that it's not right to put the marriage first because our kids are so important to us. However, think about the number of married couples walking the planet right now who don't have a clue how to create an extraordinary marriage filled with connection, passion, intimacy, and epic communication.

I'm going to share an eye-opening statistic that will really hammer the point home that it's so important that we are married first and parents second. As I mentioned before, everyone knows that the divorce rate in the US is 50 percent. What you might not know are some scary statistics about the couples that stay together. The 50 percent of couples that stay together are actually divided up equally into three different camps. I hope you are sitting down for this breakdown.

The first camp: the couple is actually happy. One third of couples that stay together can actually define their relationship as working. It's everything they ever wanted. They love each other. They communicate well. They pursue each other and date each other regularly. They have sex often. They are truly satisfied with the relationship, and it's working well. That's not say that there aren't problems or issues that arise every no w and again, but overall, the relationship is solid.

The second camp: The couple settled. We all know this couple. Chances are we might even have close friends that are in this camp. The next one third of couples are simply settling for the marriage they are in. It isn't everything they completely wanted, but it's too much work and most likely too much hassle to break the marriage up. In this camp couples find themselves more in the partnership loop (more on this later). They might be decent friends, but usually little to no intimacy. In all fairness, most couples in this camp want to move out of this and into camp one. They usually have no idea where to start and get overwhelmed by the process of recreating a close intimate relationship. The idea of trying to rekindle the relationship can be terrifying. Couples who are in this camp are in limbo. They are also somewhat terrified to try and rekindle the relationship for fear that it will be realized by both individuals that their marriage was never really meant to be. So instead of taking action, most couples are motivated to stay stagnant in camp two. This is truly unfortunate because usually with a little guidance, a map, and some accountability, the couple can easily move to camp one with a few minor tweaks to the relationship. Unfortunately, most couples won't take the step or risk to try to improve the situation. So, they stay in this camp for the duration of their relationship.

Camp three: they both want out. The final one third of married couples that stay together are absolutely miserable. They are physically, emotionally, and intimately completely disconnected. They are two individuals who live under the same roof but have completely separate lives. According to research, there are two main reasons couples in this camp actually stay married. First, the financial impact of divorce, as well as health insurance benefits potentially lost, is too risky to put ink on a divorce decree. Second, some of these couples feel it would be too devastating on the kids to break up the family. In essence, they are staying together for the kids. The interesting thing about this perception is that it could easily be one of the most devastating to the kids long term. Whether we realize it or not, our kids are extremely perceptive. They know full well when things are operating well in the marriage. Depending on their age, they may or may not be able to put words around it to describe what is going on, but they know full well something isn't right. The argument can also be made that if we are in this camp, the chances of our kids following in our footsteps with the same situation is extremely high. Our kids learn relationship skills from us. They watch us. They learn by example. When they are older, they reflect back on what they saw from their own experiences growing up. We see this all the time with parenting styles. Many of us repeat the same style of parenting our parents did with us.

The drift can be a devastating factor in our lives. It's the settling for mediocrity in our relationships, mindset, finances, health, and even zest for life. The drift is elusive and can sneak into our lives without us even knowing it. Most of us view our mediocre lives, marriages, relationships, and finances with the perception that "this is the way life is supposed to be." Well, I have news for you. It's not the way it's supposed to be, and it doesn't have to be this way for you, not if you don't want it to.

The most effective way to interrupt the drift is to take ACTION and GROW.

4 THE FIVE DIMENSIONS OF MANHOOD/ FATHERHOOD/ HUSBANDHOOD

> *"A man once asked his father, 'Father, how will I ever find the right woman?' His father replied, 'Forget finding the right woman. Focus on being the right man.'"*
>
> — Unknown

Over the past ten years, I have spent thousands of hours nose to nose and toes to toes with married men who have a deep desire to elevate their lives and step fully into their potential. It has literally been the most amazing work I have been called to do. I have heard thousands of stories from men in our mastermind, high-level people I've interviewed on the podcast, and one-on-one clients. I have gotten to know the minds, hearts, and souls of men. I have heard men share their deepest wounds, things they have never told anyone. I have heard men share what they truly want out of their marriage and the unconditional love they have for their wives. Men have shared what they are most challenged with and how they just can't seem to find a way to pursue what they truly want in life. Men have shared their deepest struggles with connecting with their kids or even anger issues because they can't seem to dial in the level of patience needed. What I can tell you about men, husbands, and fathers in general is that what we truly want are the simplest things in life. Not many men in the world are looking to make millions of dollars, drive the nicest car, live in the best house on the block, or conquer the world. What we truly want is to conquer our own world. We want to dominate our lives and live legendary on our own terms. Most men simply want to go to their graves knowing they had an extraordinary marriage and epic connection with their kids. Most of us simply want to make an impact on the people who mean the most to us. When it comes to married men with kids, our entire world truly revolves in five dimensions.

Dimension 1: Cultivating a Fulfilling Marriage

If you get to the heart and soul of any man and ask him what he wants in his marriage, he will most likely share themes around connection, intimacy, appreciation, fun, and respect. According to recent studies, there is a divorce in America every 13 seconds. Over a 40-year period, approximately 67% of marriages will terminate.[1]

I have no statistics to prove this next statement, but I honestly feel that no one gets married with the intention to get divorced. We get married because we truly want to spend our lives with

---

1. Wilkinson & Finkbeiner Family Law Attorneys, "Divorce Statistics: Over 115 Studies, Facts, and Rates for 2022, www.wf-lawyers.com. April 2022.

the woman we fell in love with. We get married because we want a marriage and a life filled with love, passion, and intimacy. No one walks down the aisle with the intention of "I can't wait to create a mediocre marriage with this person!" We get married because we want to have it all! We deeply desire to share our most authentic selves with our wives. We also want her to share her most authentic self with us.

We could make a laundry list of reasons why we perceive our relationships aren't working. We blame the other person. We aren't getting the sex and intimacy that we truly need, want, and desire. There is emotional resentment on one side or both because expectations aren't being fulfilled. She doesn't feel seen, heard, or connected to you. You don't feel respected or appreciated. You don't intentionally love her in her love language. She doesn't love you in your love language. This list could literally take up the next 10 pages if we wanted. But instead of focusing on everything that is wrong with marriages and why the majority of them don't work, what if we focused on what it takes to create the marriage of our dreams? As couples and individuals, we tend to focus on everything that is wrong and needs to be fixed, but what we resist will persist, and what we focus on becomes our reality.

Do you want to know the secret to an extraordinary marriage? Here it is... Loving each other is a choice. Connection, intimacy, passion, and optimal communication are SKILLS, not feelings. Most of us think that the dynamics of marriage are feelings. They aren't. There are definitely feelings involved; however, we need to learn skills. Skills are where the rubber meets the road. We need to learn communication skills. We need to learn skills like tactical empathy, emotional validation, mirroring, labeling, active listening, connection, creating an environment of psychological safety, and conflict resolution. Most of us assume that communication should come natural to us because we love the other person. This isn't the case. Optimal communication encompasses all of the skills listed above, and we need to know all of them.

It's also important to truly understand the four pillars of an extraordinary marriage: self-care, partnership, friendship, and lovers. These four pillars stand firmly (or weakly) on a foundation of optimal communication skills. Most of us try to navigate marriage on feelings and emotions alone. When we do that, we are setting our relationships up for dire consequences. The statistics on divorce and unhappy married couples prove that. We will dive into the deep end with both feet later in this book to help you really hone these skills and deepen the connection with your wife.

One final point before we move on to the next dimension. Think about what you do for a living. How much time and training have you put into your career? How much training did you get before you jumped into your job with both feet? The average police officer invests approximately 13 to 19 weeks of training before they are officially a police officer.[2] It takes approximately 13 years of education and training to be a general surgeon.[3] It takes over 600 hours to be a firefighter.[4] According to statistics, the average couple will spend 200 to 300 hours of preparation for the wedding day for an engagement lasting 18 months.[5] It's safe to say that most couples don't even spend a fraction of that time getting preparing for the marriage. Yet, for some crazy reason, we expect that our marriages should thrive.

2. "How Long Does It Take to Become a Police Officer?" Golawenforcement.com, 2022.
3. Jenifer Whitlock, "What Is a Surgeon?" VeryWellHealth.com, November 23, 2021.
4. Indeed Editorial Team, "FAQ: How Long Does It Take to Become a Firefighter?"
5. Alyssa Brown, "A Professional Wedding Planner Tells All: How Much Time Does It Really Take to Plan a Wedding?" MarthaStewart.com, March 11, 2021.

THE FACTS:

- Creating an extraordinary marriage doesn't happen by accident. It happens when two people are willing to learn skills to connect and create depth to the relationship.

- The feeling of love is not enough alone. Love is an action and a choice. Love is extremely important and foundational. However, love will not conquer all.

- Most people will put more time and planning into the wedding day compared to the marriage. A successful marriage needs the same. It needs planning, communication, and alignment.

- More communication within your marriage will not necessarily solve issues; *effective* communication will. Many couples think that if they have more communication, they can master communication issues, but learning specific skills like empathy and active listening, asking solution-based questions, and seeking clarity are critical to effective communication in marriage.

- Most couples do not have alignment on foundational elements in their marriage like sex, finances, faith, education, and parenting. Make sure you and your wife are aligned on all of the above. This book will give you a solid compass for exploring these.

Dimension 2: Physical, Mental, Emotional, and Spiritual Health Optimization

The health dimension encompasses four pillars of optimal health. Physical health is obviously the physical exercise of our bodies. Our bodies were designed for movement. We were never meant to be sedentary creatures. Unfortunately, the majority of our society is not only sedentary, but the majority of professional careers involve long hours sitting in front of screens for 8 to 10 hours per day. According to the CDC, only 23% of Americans get the minimum requirements for physical exercise per week. The federal physical activity guidelines suggest that adults between the ages of 18 and 64 get at least 150 minutes of exercise per week.[6] What I can tell you in my experience working with men over the years is that physical self-care is one of the first things to go when we tie the knot. Again, men give this up out of a perception of nobility and being selfless. Most men won't take the time to physically take care of themselves because we have a perception that we are being selfish if we take time away from our families or places of work for something as simple as exercise.

Our physical health is also a direct result of the food we are eating. Most Americans eat a diet that is heavy in processed foods with little to no nutritional value. We are lacking micronutrients (vitamins and minerals) in our diet that have a direct effect our on physical health. Many of us believe that this is just the way we are supposed to eat in today's society without really understanding the massive impact nutrition has on every aspect of our lives. We are filling our bodies with low-grade processed fuel. If we simply incorporate high-octane, non-processed, healthier fuel, it will have a massive impact on everything we do, from our energy levels, our appearance, even our sex drive!

"Emotional health" is often used interchangeably with "mental health," but there are notable differences. Firstly, emotional health relates specifically to social and emotional competencies, such as the ability to empathize or regulate emotions. Emotional health

---

6. Anthony Dominic, "Only 23 Percent of Americans Meet National Exercise Guidelines," ClubIndustry.com, July 5, 2018.

is having both an awareness of your emotions and the ability to manage and express those feelings in an age-appropriate manner. Mental health, on the other hand, also encompasses cognitive and neurological functioning, including things like memory and impulse control. Some mental health conditions, such as depression or anxiety, have a strong social and emotional basis, whereas others, such as dementia and autism, have more organic and neurological roots. An important distinction between mental and emotional health is that you can experience mental health issues while maintaining good emotional health and vice versa. For example, you could be struggling with a mental health problem like having very little energy for daily tasks yet still exhibit emotional health by finding effective ways to manage that lack of energy.

Just because emotional and mental health are different factors in one's life doesn't mean they aren't connected. Emotional health involves a specific collection of "assets," or social and emotional skills, which are associated a range of positive life outcomes, including reduced mental health issues. These components of emotional health aren't fixed or inherent but can be worked on and improved through self-growth and targeted support.

Emotional health support is beneficial for everyone, whether they have a mental health condition or not. There are no quick fixes for bettering our emotional health; however, there are steps we can take to improve it. For example, one tactic for improving emotional health is to identify positive situations and work on developing our strengths instead of constantly focusing on our perceived weaknesses. Men are notorious for constantly focusing on what we need to improve and where our weaknesses lie versus doubling down on our strengths. This is pretty common with human nature in general. And this is a sure-fire way to damage our emotional health over time. One of the ways we can stay emotionally healthy is being proactive with seeking help, mentorships, and guidance. We can do this through a variety of ways, such as joining a men's group at church, hiring a coach, seeing a counselor, or joining a mastermind. At the very least, having a standing monthly coffee/breakfast with a trusted friend or mentor can do wonders for emotional health. Keep in mind, isolation is the enemy of excellence. Having likeminded individuals or mentors in your life will make a world of difference.

Again, just like physical health, men tend to ignore their mental and emotional health. Society does a great job at setting men for failure in this realm. Most men won't reach out and ask for help when their mental or emotional health is seriously challenged. The suicide rates in our country today prove this point. According to the Centers of Disease Control and Prevention, the second leading cause of death for men 25 to 35 is suicide.[7] For men between the ages of 35 and 54, suicide is the third leading cause of death. There are several factors that contribute to these outcomes, which we will delve into further in this book.

The final pillar for optimal health is our spiritual health. I am a Christian and I am open about my faith. Spiritual health can mean different things to different people. Believe it or not, there are over 10,000 distinct religions in the world. Approximately 84 percent of the world's population is affiliated with Christianity, Islam, Hinduism, or Buddhism. Spiritual health includes the belief in a purposeful life. It can also mean the transcendence and actualization of different dimensions and capabilities of human beings. Spiritual health creates a balance between physical, psychological, and social aspects of our lives.

---

7. Daniel C. Ehlman, Deborah M. Stone, Christopher M. Jones and Karin A. Mack, "Changes in Suicide Rates – United States, 2019 and 2020," *Morbidity and Mortality Weekly Report* (MMWR) 71, 8 (2022): 306 – 312.

THE FACTS:

- When it comes to taking care of our physical bodies, most men will put this critical need on the backburner because they perceive they don't have time, that it's selfish, or it simply isn't important enough to invest the time.

- When it comes to mental and emotional health, there are distinct differences. Make sure you take time to fulfill both.

- Most men will lone wolf life without a tribe of good men surrounding them who have their best interests at the helm. Isolation is the enemy of excellence. Isolation will negatively impact your journey as a man, husband, and father. As a result, isolation will have a huge negative impact on your emotional and mental health.

- You are the spiritual leader of your family. Whether you believe in a higher power or not, your family (especially your kids) will look to you as their compass for their spiritual life.

Dimension 3: Mastering Your Personal/Family Finances

A survey by Salary Finance conducted over recent years showed nearly 50 percent of employees reported high levels of stress and anxiety due to finances.[8] According to a Morgan and Stanley study, 78% of employees have reported that their level of financial stress has become a major distraction in the workplace.[9] The larger a

---

8. "Is Financial Stress Affecting Your Workplace? Find Out in Minutes," Neighborhood Trust Financial Partners, NeighborhoodTrust.org, 2022.
9. iGrad Author, "The Secret to Conquering Employee Financial Stress," The Well: A Financial Wellness Blog by the Authors at Enrich, Enrich.org, April 20, 2022.

couple's debt, the more likely they were to say money is one of the top issues they fight about. We won't be diving deep into this topic in the book, as giving financial advice is not my area of expertise. However, I will say that this is a real problem, and optimizing your financial vision and future is a must when it comes to living a legendary life. One of the biggest issues we face is that the majority of married adults have never taken a personal finance course. We are simply winging it and hoping for the best. Unfortunately, winging it is not a strategy.

THE FACTS:[10]

- Nearly half of marriages end because of misalignment on family finances.

- Only 30% of US households have a long-term financial plan. This alone can be devastating to the long-term financial vision of the family.

- 20% of Americans do not save any part of their annual income

- 42% of Americans have less than $10,000 saved for retirement.

- Personal finance stats show that 39% of Americans would have trouble covering an unexpected cash expense of just $400.

Dimension 4: Epic Connection and Patience with Kids

Ask nearly any man, and he will tell you that being a father is one of the most important aspects of his life. Being a father is epic and humbling at the same time. Men treasure time with their kids. It's so important to us that we raise good human beings

---

10. I. Mitic, "What Happened to Your Paycheck? Personal Finance Statistics for 2022," Fortunly, March 18, 2022.

but not *just* raise them; we want to do life with them as well. Men desperately want to have a connection with their kids that goes far beyond a surface-level relationship. We want depth. We want memories. We want connection. We want to be their go-to for everything. We want to teach them life lessons and positive character traits. We want to coach their sporting teams. The dads of this generation WANT MORE! We are seeing a generation of fathers that are hungrier for connection and depth compared to generations past. I'm not saying our fathers did things completely wrong. However, back in the 40s, 50s, 60s, 70s, 80s, and even the 90s, fathers viewed their roles as providers primarily. They simply didn't have the resources that are available today to dive a little deeper. Not to mention, their generation of fathers raised them with even more of an emphasis on being a provider. Today, we are seeing a surge of dads step up, raise their hands, and say, "I WANT MORE!" We are seeing more hands-on dads today than ever before. This is amazing!

The problem that we face is that most of us still believe that parenting should come naturally to us. We think and feel that we shouldn't get angry and lose our patience. We desperately want to connect on a deep level with our kids, but at times, it seems impossible. We might not have the connection and the depth that we truly want. Moreover, we don't know how to get more depth and connection with our kids. At times, parenting can feel like we are in a dark room, alone, filled with obstacles that we can't see, searching for the light switch. With every step we take or every attempt to find the light switch, we find ourselves stubbing our toe or tripping over something. It can be frustrating, and some days it can feel extremely defeating.

Just like creating an extraordinary marriage is a skill, so is parenting. Connection, communication, creating more patience, and creating an environment of psychological safety are all skills. Again, most of us are under the impression that parenting should come naturally. It doesn't. The love we have for our kids comes naturally, but the skills are things we need to learn. During times of extreme frustration with our kids, we aren't necessarily frustrated with our kids. We are actually frustrated with ourselves. Kids will be kids. They will be imperfect and act out. They will test us. They will act in ways that only a drunk person would. Good parenting doesn't come from our kids never acting out and living perfect lives. Good parenting happens in how we respond to our environment and situations with our kids. Most of the time, we have the best of intentions when our kids test us. Unfortunately, most of us react and do not create space to respond. Reaction and response are different. Reaction is more of a knee-jerk reaction to a situation, and a response is calmer, more collected, and much more intentional.

We (dads) are extremely hard on ourselves. We can self-sabotage and be incredibly critical of ourselves when we are being tested. At times, the most lethal bully in our lives is the voice between our two ears that only we can hear. When our kids test us (and they always will), at times, we can react in anger. We can lash out. We can yell and scream. We then get angry and disappointed in ourselves and our reaction. We start telling ourselves how awful we are and that we don't know what we are doing. We not only get angry with our kids for being kids, but we also get angry at ourselves. We start questioning our self-worth. We start to question if we are even up to the challenge of being a parent. It can be a really nasty road of self-sabotage. At the end of the day, we are extremely hard on ourselves, which can make our journey as a parent extremely difficult. Being a parent is difficult. However, it's up to us to learn new skills and grow so that bad times are minimal and the good times are maximized.

This goes back to all of the examples above of professions that require hours, weeks, months, and years of training. Yet when it comes to being a parent, the average mom and dad spend under five hours prepping for parenthood before having their first child. To add insult to injury, most of us don't do continuing education like parenting classes, conferences, mentorship, coaching, counseling, or masterminds because we feel if we need to ask for advice, we are weak and not up to the task of parenting. This is one of the biggest lies we tell ourselves. Gents, take it from me, parenting is so much more enjoyable when you know how to do the next right thing. Take that from a man who struggled with being a father for nearly the first ten years of my kids' lives. I was lost. I had no clue what to do in most situations, and I was frustrated I didn't know the way. It wasn't until l surrendered to several facts that were always true and staring me right in the face that I began to find my way.

THE FACTS:

- Parenting is a SKILL, and the skill doesn't come naturally. The love for our kids comes naturally but not the skills needed.

- Patience is a SKILL, not a feeling. Human beings by nature are not patient creatures. The good news is we can learn the skill of patience and put it into practice.

- Creating an environment of psychological safety where our kids will talk to us about just about anything is a SKILL.

- We don't have to do this alone. Men, in general, lone wolf their lives. We are the average of the five people we spend the most time with. It's critical to always spend time with other growth-minded men who elevate us and elevate them in return.

- Parenting is an imperfect journey. We will never achieve mistake-free parenting. We will screw up. We are human. How we recover from mistakes is the most important aspect of making mistakes.

- No matter how old we are or how old our kids are, we can always learn how to connect with them. It's never too late.

Dimension 5: Leadership

If you are a father, you are in a leadership role—I would argue the most important leadership role we will have. We are leading our kids, our businesses (or places of work), our wives, our finances, and ourselves. No one would disagree with the fact that leadership is a skill. What we will spend most of the time in this book exploring is how we can lead ourselves so we can selflessly serve and lead others in a more profound way. There are six essential skills for men/husbands/fathers in this book that are critical for effective leadership.

First, an influential leader is someone who knows how to be supportive. Some of the best leaders are available (physically, mentally, and emotionally) to the people that mean the most to them. They create an environment of support and empathy. They are focused on creating a culture of growth and positive morale.

Second, a great leader has high emotional intelligence. Emotional intelligence and empathy are the new currencies for the best leaders. If you truly want to create connection and safety, we have to make sure the people who mean the most to us (our families) feel seen and heard. People are more likely follow and be inspired by someone when they feel heard, seen, and connected in a safe environment.

Third, clear communication is critical for a great leader. Clear communication is a two-way street. Many of us would define optimal communication as being able to say what we need to say very clearly so everyone understands. However, clear communication is both being an effective listener and being able to clearly speak. In fact, some of the best communicators do the least amount of talking. Instead, they know how to ask really good questions to empower others to think deeper.

Fourth, a great leader can make decisions quickly. Many of us are stricken with a condition called "analysis paralysis." Not making a decision at all can be more detrimental than making a poor decision. At least when we make poor decisions, we can debrief, learn, and pivot. Great leaders gather essential information and then make decisions quickly.

Fifth, great leaders collaborate. No one likes to follow a dictator, and if they do, they will most likely be resentful. They might follow someone who is a dictator for a certain period of time, but usually their morale, performance, and connection to the dictator is extremely strained. Disclaimer, as a father, there is definitely a time and place where you might have to be the dictator. There are times and places where we need to enforce rules and it's black and white. However, keep in mind, during the times it doesn't have to be black and white, we can include our families in small decisions, big decisions, plans for the future, how we connect as a family, activities that we do together, and how we create connection with each other.

Sixth, leadership is a skill we can learn, implement, and put into practice. Leaders are lifelong learners. They are curious about people, connection, and learning new things, and they always ask good questions of themselves and people around them. Some of us are more natural leaders than others, but all of us can learn how to be a more effective leader.

When we really pull back the curtain on what is in the minds and hearts of men, husbands, and fathers, the five dimensions listed above reveal themselves. When we are open to learning skills to optimize these domains, our journeys as fathers and husbands become more fulfilling. Throughout the rest of this book, we will take a deep dive into the simple and tangible skill sets that you can learn quickly and implement effectively to become the best husband, father, and leader you can be.

PART 2
HUSBAND

5 CREATING AN EXTRAORDINARY MARRIAGE

> *"A successful marriage isn't based on the length of time we are together. It's based on the strong foundation we build together."*
>
> — Larry Hagner

As I reflect upon my childhood, there was a common theme of would-be father figures that would come in and out of my life. By the time I was just 12 years old, I lost my biological father twice and my stepdad. My mom would continue to date different men over the years and between marriages. By the time I was 20 years old, she had been married three times and had several failed relationships.

I'm not going to use this book to share the journey of failed relationships I saw my mom go through, but I will tell you it had a massive impact on my life.

My mother's marriage with Joe came to an end when I was 10 years old. When he moved out of the house, I remember feeling torn because a part of me was relieved that there would be no more fighting. There wouldn't be any more drunken outbursts. I wouldn't have to worry about waking up in the middle of the night and seeing them physically and emotionally inflicting harm on each other. I would no longer be concerned about Joe hitting me out of anger. The tension in the house between them would be gone. I felt good. I was relieved.

On the flip side, I also felt uncertainty and a tremendous void in my life. *Who will teach me about being a man? Who will teach me how to fix things? Who will be there to play catch with me? If it's just me and Mom, how will we make sure we have enough money to survive?* Abandonment will definitely leave a child feeling unsettled and uncertain about the next steps.

My mom went on to date a few different men over the next couple of years. All of them were basically the same man, just a different face and name. All of the men that came into my life over the next two years were partiers, drinkers, and really didn't want much to do with me.

When I was 12, I had the opportunity to unexpectedly meet my biological father for the first time, and it would turn into a six-month relationship. I was overjoyed to meet him, and during the six months I knew my dad, we spent time regularly. He was remarried at the time. He had a two-year-old son and another one on the way. He is still married to the same woman today, and they have been together over 40 years. There was always a sense of stability being over at their house. No one really drank heavily. No one got mad and screamed at anyone. There was always a sense of peace under their roof. Towards the end of our sixth-month relationship, I remember feeling a sense that he was overwhelmed with something, but I could never figure out what it was. I just remember it was a feeling of heaviness when we were together. Our relationship came to an end at that sixth-month mark, and it didn't end well. To be honest, I don't really remember what was said during our last conversation. I only remember my dad being feeling torn and he wasn't sure how to navigate this new part of his life. I was angry and I remember hanging up the phone. That was our last conversation for the next 18 years.

By the time I was 12, I had lost my biological father twice and lost my stepfather. It was a difficult time in my life, and I just gave up. I emotionally overate and gained a lot of weight. Athletics really didn't help because I wasn't the most coordinated youth athlete; however, I did play baseball and basketball.

Between the age of 12 and 15, men came and went from my mom's life. Some I only met once. Some would stick around for a season. Some would stick around for a year. They all started the same and ended the same.

My mom met another man when I was 15 that would be the most dysfunctional relationship I saw growing up. The relationship started out just like all the others—with excitement and happiness. They moved really fast, and within a matter of months, he and his son (who was also my age) moved into our house. Suddenly, after just months of dating, we were now a somewhat oddly blended family. His son was one of the most toxic people I have ever met. He had a criminal record. He was into drugs and gang activity. At one point, he even held a knife up to my neck and threatened to kill me in my sleep if I told my mom and his dad he was doing drugs. Our blended family would stay under the same roof for the next 12 months. It was the worst and most toxic year of my life up to that point. So many nights were filled with a ton of alcohol, which would lead to fun at first but then explode into fights and madness.

There was always immense excitement at the beginning of every new relationship. My mom (and whoever she was dating) seemed on top of the world. The environment in the house always seemed happy and positive during those times. As time went on in the relationship, I saw the same patterns emerge over and over. I saw several things that I know destroy most marriages and even the best-intended relationships. I saw poor communication, unfulfilled expectations, emotional resentment, yelling, disrespect, name calling, the silent treatment, avoidance, physical abuse, extreme reactivity, loss of patience, and much more.

This all sounds like doom and gloom, and to be honest, there was a lot of that. However, it was also one of the best educations I could possibly ask for growing up because it was an example of what not to do. There were so many times in my life when I used my past hardships growing up as an excuse to play the victim role in many areas of my life.

Many of us have stories of our childhoods. We have memories that we experienced and things that we witnessed with our parents. Some memories are positive, and some aren't. Some of us remember the majority of our experiences growing up as chaos while others remember more good times.

Those memories are neither bad nor good; they just are. Where the rubber meets the road is what we do with those memories and stories. Do we use them to lean on a story of the victim and why we can't be successful in our own marriages and relationships? Or do we take the learnings from the good and bad to make the life, marriage, and relationships we always wanted? It's truly up to us.

As you read through the following chapters in this part of the book, we will go over several skill sets that will set you up for more success versus more failure and frustration in your marriage.

6 THE SECRET NO ONE TELLS YOU ABOUT MARRIAGE

> "The secret to a happy marriage is if you can be at peace with someone within four walls, if you are content because the one you love is near to you, either upstairs or downstairs, or in the same room, and you feel that warmth that you don't find often, then that is what love is all about."
>
> — Bruce Forsyth

Creating an extraordinary involves learning skills. Believe it or not, that is the secret. Many of us believe that an extraordinary marriage happens on its own or it will somehow just evolve into something we have always dreamed of simply because we love each other. That doesn't happen. The feeling of love doesn't conquer all. Loving each other is obviously a must and extremely important, but creating connection, intimacy, and depth of communication with your wife doesn't happen unless you are willing to learn how to do those things.

Perhaps in reading the above paragraph there was a part of you that this didn't sit well with. Maybe you're even a bit pissed off at that fact that these things don't happen on their own, but again, I want you to think about how much training goes into certain jobs in our society.

As I mentioned before, it takes 13 to 19 weeks of training for the average police recruit to become a sworn officer. Men and women who serve and protect go into this line of work because they have a desire and maybe even a love of the idea of serving their community. We wouldn't expect that a police cadet simply becomes an officer on the first day they show up for the job. We expect that they go through a rigorous training program to ensure they can do the job effectively. The love of the job alone doesn't cut it. There is a huge commitment of training and learning new skills to be able to do that job. Yet in our marriages we walk down the aisle with the best of intentions, and we truly believe everything will be OK and even extraordinary just because we love each other.

One more example before we move on. The average surgeon must go through at least eight years of education, then two years of residency, and a further two years of fellowship before they are set free to start their own practice. We wouldn't think of being cut open on the OR table by a surgeon who wasn't highly trained and skilled. We would never be operated on by someone who simply showed up to the job that first day and maybe even got a certificate online stating that they passed the required online course to do open heart surgery. Yet when we open our heart up to another person who we want to be with for the rest of our lives, many of us don't do any work to learn how to be married. We don't take the time before or even during the relationship to do the deep work individually or as a couple so we can connect the way we were meant to connect. Yet we wonder why the divorce rate is 50 percent.

Is this making sense yet?

Maybe at this point a few light bulbs have turned on. Think about it for a minute. Everything in life that we are required to do well takes training, work, and learning new skills to perform. Think of your job. Think of the professional athletes you see on TV. Think of the teachers that teach your kids. Think of the doctor you see when you are sick. We fully expect that in order for us to operate at an elite level, there are skills, practice, and training that are required. Yet we don't have this view of our marriages. In fact, many of us have the opposite view! If we need help or even counseling, we assume that we are broken, weak, or something is seriously wrong with us. I get it. I was there too. It's time to eradicate this belief from every married couple out there.

7 THE 4 ELEMENTS OF AN EXTRAORDINARY MARRIAGE

> *"The difference between an ordinary marriage and an extraordinary marriage is in giving just a little extra every day, as long as possible, for as long as we both shall live."*
>
> — Fawn Weaver

In 2018, there was an amazing book written by Lance and Brandy Salazar with Hal Elrod called *The Miracle Morning for Couples*. Many of you probably know the impact that Hal Elrod has had on millions of lives with his original book and now several installments of *The Miracle Morning* series.

If you are married, *The Miracle Morning for Couples* is a must read. Most of us know what marriage looks like and feels like from a 30,000-foot view. But what is it really made of when you get into to weeds and details? What do extraordinary couples do that other couples don't? What makes a legendary marriage versus a marriage that survives?

According to Lance and Brandy, the four elements of a legendary marriage are self-care, partnership, friends, and lovers. Imagine these four elements sitting on a foundation of solid communication. When it comes to communication, when asked what we want more of, we usually respond with to adjectives. We want "more and/or better."

Many of us will say, "I want better communication with my wife" or "I want more communication with my wife." Everyone wants "more and better communication," but very few can tell us how. "More and better" don't give us specifics of the "how." "More and better" doesn't even define the desired end state. How do we even know we have achieved more and better if we don't even know what more and better looks like?

We don't settle for "more and better" in other areas of our life, so why would we settle for it in our marriage?

Think about the last time you went to the doctor for a physical or even some bloodwork. After looking over the bloodwork or after doing the physical, your doctor says, "I need you to go get healthier."

Your next question would most likely be "What's wrong?" and then "What do I need to do?"

What if your doctor responded with: "Don't even worry about it; just go get healthier"?

You might start asking deeper questions like: "Do I have a cholesterol issue? Do I have cancer? Do I have diabetes? Do I have a heart issue?" Your mind would be racing with the specific thing you would have to do to get healthier.

What if your doctor responded once again: "Don't even worry about it; I just want you to get in better health"?

You can see where "more and better" aren't razor focused and we have no idea what to do if it's so general.

In order to have connected communication with your wife, you must develop several skill sets and practice them over and over. The communication skills we will go over are skills that the majority of married couples never learn or even grasp the meaning of. In order to communicate effectively, we have to learn skills like tactical empathy, emotional validation, labels, mirrors, active listening, and even creating an environment of psychological safety. Before we jump into the specifics of these tactics, let's start with the four elements.

Element #1: Self-Care

At the foundation of a man's heart is nobility. Not only nobility but selflessness. Most men want to serve their wives and kids. We want to provide, protect, and lead. We are willing to sacrifice ourselves to do these things. In fact, we do this to an absolute extreme. After we get married and have children, our self-care becomes one of our last priorities (if not the last). We perceive we can give more if we don't take time, effort, and resources to take care of ourselves.

Most men will work more hours every week so they can provide more. Some of us are working 70, 80, even 90 hours a week or more so we can provide more means. We don't take any time away for ourselves to attend to our mental, emotional, physical, and even spiritual needs. We perceive this as selfless and noble. To some degree it is. A man who works hard for his family is noble. A man who then works hard and long hours to spend the leftover time with his family, leaving none for himself is noble to some degree, but at what cost? When we are pulling hours like this in the workplace and spending what little time we have remaining with the family, are we showing up in the best way possible

- Stress reduction
- The feeling of vibrance and health
- Physical, mental, and emotional well-being
- Improved patience and emotional resilience when we go through stressful times
- Overall feeling of increased happiness and fulfillment

Let's break down some simple physical self-care.
- Walk for 15 minutes outside
- Go for a 25-minute run
- Grab some workout time at the gym for 45 – 60 minutes, three times per week
- Do 50 burpees (takes about 2 to 5 minutes)
- Do 20 pushups at the top of every hour before lunch (takes about 30 to 60 seconds per hour)
- YouTube a 15-minute ab routine
- Play on a sports league just one night a week for an hour
- Hire an online trainer to create a program that is built around your busy schedule
- Jump into a sauna for 15 minutes
- Take a cold shower (enjoyable for some, misery for others) for three minutes
- Incorporate your kids into your workouts by going outside and playing a sport for 30 minutes to an hour over the weekend
- Go for a hike with your wife
- Workout with your wife before you go out on a date night
- Play a sport with your wife
- Get a workout partner

Here's the deal—the benefits of doing something physical for self-care far outweigh the cons. We also don't have to commit long hours to reap the benefits. When we look at the amount of time the above activities take from our day, it's not much compared to the 1,440 minutes we are all given every single day.

Let's break down mental and emotional health. Before we do that, let's first acknowledge that at times it's uncomfortable for many men to talk about mental health or emotions. But here is the bottom line: if you want to operate at a high level, your mental and emotional well-being is critical. The more we try to stuff issues, problems, and stress down and not deal with it, the more issues we will have in our lives. That's not to say that now we have to become soft, weeping, feminine wet sponges. We simply have to acknowledge we are human beings that feel emotions. We are a walking, talking conversation with ourselves that experiences the highs and lows of mental space and emotional roller coasters. Emotions are neither bad nor good; they just are. If we feel sad, we should honor that we need to feel sad. If we feel angry or frustrated, we need to honor that as well. If we feel happiness and bliss, we need to honor those good feelings. Our emotions make us human beings. Emotions alone don't make us weak or inferior men. Emotions just are.

On the flip side, if our emotions dictate our every action or every inaction, that is where we could have issues. Our emotional states can dictate a swift, hardcore reaction or a steady response. Our emotions can dictate whether we act promptly or are paralyzed. This is why emotional control is just as important as feeling our emotions.

What would our lives look like if we simply allowed ourselves to feel our emotions, but we could think logically about decisions?

Have you ever felt like not doing something, but you did it anyway despite not feeling like it? Maybe the feeling of frustration came over you when it was time to go to the gym and exercise.

Maybe you didn't feel like going because your day was hard or stressful. Maybe you felt like staying home, that you would enjoy yourself more there, but instead you made the choice to go exercise despite the feeling of dread or even zero motivation. You simply took action despite your feelings. You went to the gym and trained hard for 30 minutes. You left feeling revived, refreshed, and even accomplished. You took the action necessary to drive the result you wanted despite not feeling like it.

Think of a time you felt anger when one of your kids lied to you or stepped out of line and you responded with calm versus reacting in rage that resulted in yelling and screaming. Despite the emotion of anger, you chose your response of calm. Maybe there was a part of you that didn't feel like being calm, yet in the moment, you were able to choose the outcome you wanted.

Think of a time when you felt annoyed towards your wife, and you responded with kindness. Perhaps you didn't feel like being kind—you felt irritated—yet in the moment, you were able to choose the outcome you wanted.

Optimizing mental and emotional health is not about ignoring what we are feeling or stuffing it down into the unknown, never dealing with it, and it's not about prioritizing our current and sometimes wayward emotions above all else. Optimal mental and emotional health is being capable of feeling whatever we are feeling and being able to choose a response to what is happening. Many of us have heard the quote: "It's not about what happens to us; it's how we respond." If we aren't taking time to take care of our mental health and be more in tune with our emotional IQ, we will continue to fall victim to knee-jerk reactions, anger, and feelings of constant high stress followed by internal self-sabotage. No one wants that.

So, how do we do it?

Sharpening our mental and emotional health needs to be a daily practice. We can do this in several different ways, but what is most important is that it becomes a practice and a habit.

Journaling

Journaling can be a powerful tool for understanding where we are mentally and emotionally. The mental, emotional, and physical act of writing our thoughts, feelings, and reflections on paper is a powerful exercise in stress reduction, clarity, and strategy. At times, it can feel like there are 20 ping pong balls just bouncing from side to side within our minds. Just reflecting on all of the thoughts and emotions that emerge for us in a day can feel overwhelming. But what if we took the time (just five minutes a day) to reflect on some of those bouncing ping pong balls? What if we took a few minutes to settle them down and identify what they were and what they meant? Journaling will not only help us to gain emotional mastery; it will improve our emotional IQ and make us better dads and husbands. When we understand our own emotions and get clarity through reflection, we are better equipped to guide loved ones through theirs.

If you want something simple, here's my daily journaling regimen.

I start with gratitude. I choose two to five things in my life that I am grateful for. Maybe I am thankful for my health. Maybe it's something as simple as being able to walk or waking up another day. Maybe I am grateful for something one of my boys said or did that brought me joy. In these moments of gratitude, I am choosing to reflect and acknowledge the good things in my life despite whatever I am dealing with that could be negative.

Next, I reflect on a challenge (or a few) that I am facing. Maybe the connection with my wife isn't where I want it to be. Perhaps there is a problem that needs urgent attention within my business. Maybe I'm dealing with a parenting challenge with one of the boys. Whatever it is, I reflect on the challenge and allow space to start thinking about solutions versus focusing on the problems.

For example: If I feel that my wife, Jessica, and I are disconnected, I don't focus on the stress and feeling of being disconnected. I don't ask myself really poor questions like: "Why aren't we connecting right now? What are we doing wrong?" When I ask myself questions like this, I will get problem based, low-quality answers back. Instead, I ask myself: "How might we elevate our connection today? How might we make each other feel loved, seen, and heard?" When I take time and space to ask myself really powerful questions like those, high-quality, solution-based answers flow. So, just make sure when you are reflecting on the challenges, use the "How might I/we..." question format versus the "Why can't I/we..." question format.

Next, I reflect on what I am most excited about for the day. When we reflect upon something good that is going to happen during our day, it puts us back into the state of gratitude. It's easy to dread the day. It's easy to dread parts of our day that might be challenging. Dinner with your family can be something you enjoy, but it can also be stressful. At times, our kitchen tables can be absolute chaos, with kids dropping food and talking over each other, or they can be uncomfortable, with kids who don't talk at all (if they are in their teenage years). However, if we can focus on the gratitude versus the chaos, it can help our mentality and improve our emotional health.

Here's an example: "*I am excited to have dinner with Jessica and the four boys tonight. I realize that dinner time might be mad chaos. The little ones will most likely drop food, make a mess, and talk over each other. The older boys might not say much at all. I may even have to remind them that we don't have our phones at the dinner table for the thousandth time. However, I choose to look forward to dinner with all of them tonight. There will come a day when our entire family isn't gathered at one dinner table. The older boys will be off to college. The younger boys might be out with friends. Jessica and I will be sitting at a table that seats six people, and it will be just the two of us. So, for tonight, I am going to embrace the chaos. I will enjoy the high energy. I will love that fact that I get to look around the table and see all of my kids' faces and hear about their day."*

Iron Sharpens Iron: Friendships for Mental and Emotional Health Optimization

Another aspect of our life that greatly influences our mental and emotional health is the circle of friends/men we choose to surround ourselves with. It's safe to say that most of us have a circle of friends. However, it's another thing to really look at the depth of those relationships.

Stephen Mansfield has written several bestselling books for men. Three of his most popular books are *Mansfield's Book of Manly Men*, *Men on Fire*, and *Building Your Band of Brothers*. In each one of these books he talks very candidly about the relationships we have with other men as we get older. When we are young, we are open to new friendships. It's actually easy to make friendships and even deep friendships. When we are in high school and college, these friendships do have depth, but not necessarily the maturity required for the marathon of life as we get older. For most men, the depth of our friendships comes to a screeching halt after we are out of college, enter the workplace, get married, and start having kids, even if we are making new friends.

Over time, we begin to lose touch with other men and old friendships in our lives. We become too busy with the obligations of work and family. The friendships we sustain into the years of us being married and having kids tend to lack any real depth. We will most likely have the same conversations with these friends over and over. We talk about work and how busy we are. We talk about our kids, their activities, and how busy our family is. We might talk about marriage, but with very little detail. We don't share about aspects of our marriage like connection, intimacy, and communication. We don't confide in our friends when we get impatient with our kids. We don't talk about our finances if we're worried about them. We certainly don't talk about our physical, mental, or emotional health. We keep it surface level and safe at all times.

Mansfield refers to these friendships as "rust relationships." The relationship is "rusty" and has no polish, glimmer, or shine. It isn't a relationship that has deep meaning or authenticity. It offers surface-level companionship, but that is about the extent of it.

Men need deep relationships with a band of brothers to truly live and thrive. They need relationships with men who elevate them to do great things in their lives. What men truly need is a circle good friends—advisors who can help them navigate life.

Asking for Help

One of the hardest things for a man to do is to ask for help. We have this preconceived notion that if we ask others for help, we are somehow weak and not up to even the simplest aspects of life. Guys, this is simply not true. It's a lie that we tell ourselves.

Back in 2018, I was interviewing an elite Navy SEAL Sniper, Chris Sajnog, on *The Dad Edge Podcast*. This man is one of the best snipers to have ever walked the earth. Not to mention the rigorous training that SEALs have to complete. Navy, Sea, Air, and Land (SEAL) training is approximately 71 weeks from entry and consists of Navy Recruit Training (8 weeks), completion of Naval

Special Warfare Preparatory School (8 weeks), Basic Underwater Demolition/SEAL Training (24 weeks), a Navy Special Warfare Parachute Course (5 weeks), and SEAL Qualification Training (26 weeks). A grand total of a little over 16 months of training to earn the Special Warfare insignia (SEAL "Trident"). It's safe to say that SEALs are one of the most elite groups of warriors on the planet. During my interview with Chris, I asked him why the SEALs are so successful. I have always been so curious about how the SEALs have been able to accomplish the impossible.

Chris's response floored me.

He said, "That's easy... We ask for help when we need it."

I was shocked. My perception of SEALs was that they were the toughest men on the planet. They could do absolutely anything. They could conquer and accomplish anything they set their minds to! *Ask for help? Why?*

Chris went on to explain, "The reason we are so successful is because we work together as a team. We have a brotherhood. The team is strong because of the individual SEALs, and the SEAL is strong because of the team. We have to communicate. We have to speak up when we need help. If we don't, we are actually doing a disservice to the entire team. If I am in need of help and I don't ask, I can't possibly do my job effectively for the team if I am in trouble. I can't possibly serve at the highest level unless I am operating at the highest level. If I need help and don't ask, I put all of us in danger."

Chris went on to talk about how he lives by the acronym TEAMS to navigate not only his military life but also life in general.

T – Take Responsibility
E – Encourage Others
A – Ask for Help
M – Manage Your Job
S – Sacrifice

Taking Responsibility

It's not always easy to do; owning our failures is hard. Not owning them, however, doesn't teach us how to better ourselves. Instead, avoiding ownership simply delays the high probability we will make the same mistake in the future.

Encourage Others

When we help others to nurture their own talents, we are helping the greater cause. Each of us has skills and gifts that support others; not one of us is completely equipped to handle it all. Encouraging others while sharpening our own talents strengthens the individual while providing a stronger outcome in any situation.

Ask For Help

It's hard, but necessary. Swallowing your pride to ask for a hand when you need it shows that you have faith in others and are confident enough in yourself to know when you need help. Asking for help also helps to avoid embarrassing pitfalls when it's clear you would have benefitted from assistance.

Master Yourself

This is critical. When we have a grip on our strengths, weaknesses, and emotions, we can handle pretty much anything. When we don't really know our true limits or how to control ourselves, our world can spiral out of control.

TEAM is not only critical for us but for those around us. Being a positive role model for our children is the best way to teach them how to be their best selves.

Sacrifice

Sacrifice is all about doing the things we might not want to necessarily do but we must for the greater good of the team. Each SEAL knows that at some point, he might have to do things that are extremely difficult to ensure success for all. SEALs are known for successfully completing the most impossible and deadly missions. They deploy from their family, home, and country and put themselves in danger. They put themselves in harm's way to defend our freedoms. Some pay the ultimate sacrifice with their own lives for their larger purpose.

The lesson here is this, when we are pinned down in life, it's critical we ask for help. The old saying of "men never stop and ask for directions" is completely false. I would argue that most men breathe a sigh of relief when we know where we are going and what we need to do. It sure beats the feeling of being completely lost.

There are two more powerful benefits to asking for help. When we ask for help from another man, we are actually showing our most authentic self. When we are our most authentic self, people that we interact with will naturally relate to us more than we think. No one relates to perfection. It's actually the opposite. The glue that holds relationships together is authenticity and vulnerability. Secondly, when we ask for help or advice, we are giving the other man permission to do the same. When we lead with authenticity and imperfection, we are actually giving the man we are speaking to the gift of authenticity. You are giving him permission to ask for help just by leading by example. The next time you are tempted to keep your struggles to yourself, remind yourself that you are actually giving a gift to someone else by giving them permission to do the same. As men, we are more alike than we think. Every man needs a battle brother. We all need men that we can go to war with. If the Navy SEALs can live by that, why can't we do the same?

When it comes to asking for help, we underestimate the power and wisdom that can be shared from other married men in our lives. We have an online community of husbands and fathers called The Dad Edge Alliance Mastermind. It was founded in 2017, and to date we have nearly 1000 members from across the globe. Our members take part in our virtual group coaching sessions on a weekly basis. Usually, we have 15 to 18 men who are on a group coaching session at a time. I've been fascinated over the years to hear men ask questions and ask for help from other men who are on the coaching sessions. At any given point, with 15 to 18 men on a call, we usually have a combined 100-plus years of marriage experience. Some have been married only a year, some for over 30 years, and everything in between. When men are able to crowdsource wisdom from other men and their experiences, it's amazing the advice and strategies that emerge from one man asking for help. When we are able to ask for help and advice from other like-minded men in our lives, it's truly remarkable how our relationships can change with very simple shifts and tweaks.

As we wrap up self-care, it's important to really understand why this is so important. We can't possibly serve or lead at the highest level unless we are taking care of ourselves at the highest level. Leaders lead and pour into others from a full cup. A burnt out, overwhelmed, and stressed-out leader doesn't make us an effective leader. It actually makes us suboptimal leader. So, make sure you take the time, energy, and resources to ensure your cup is full and ready to lead.

Element #2: Partnership

The second element of creating an extraordinary marriage is partnership. In order for your marriage to thrive and flourish, creating real friendship and intimacy, you need to get some of the basics right. Partnership is the business side of your relationship. It is the environment you create together and for your family. It is making money, budgeting, saving, planning for the future, and all other financial aspects of life. Partnership is the daily running of your lives: roles, chores, laundry, cooking, shuttling kids, and all the rest. It is the values, goals, dreams, and alignment of your relationship "compass" pointing in the same direction. It is no surprise that this area is where most arguments happen and in the throes of marital crisis is where many marriages end. "You didn't do this, I always do that, this didn't get done at all, and I can't believe we forgot to…" Couples get overwhelmed in the Partnership Loop™ with the milelong to-do lists, lack of financial alignment and communication, and overly packed family calendar (you know, kept in their heads and hardly ever written down) and feel like there is never enough time to get it done.

The foundational principles of being aligned partners are:

- **Values** – People experience greater fulfillment when they live in alignment with their values. Our values are the things we consider most important in our lives. They are part of us. They highlight what we stand for. At the end of this book, there is a Core Values Exercise that I encourage you to check out. It will help you to get clear on what matters to you most. Share it with your wife, as well, and see what values you share as a couple!

- **Roles** – If we consider what makes a successful business partnership work, each partner comes with specific strengths and experiences. You need to know what you're good at and what your role is in the business of your marriage. We all have strengths, and we need to play to them.

- **Finances** – This isn't about how to make a million bucks. It's about honest, open, and completely transparent communication about your financial situation. It's about understanding each other's money style, creating a budget, and setting times to check in on status.

- **Parenting** – The two of you must get on the same page about how you will parent your children. Next to money, this can be what most couples fight about. Instilling values, education, discipline, etc.—it all requires strong communication and a plan.

- **Home/Schedules** – These are nuts/bolts and systems. Chores, maintenance, menu, groceries, and calendars.

We all have expectations of our spouse. It's human nature to expect that our spouses will operate in a certain way that is aligned with how we operate. When those expectations are not being met, we tend to get resentful. When emotional resentment starts to build without being addressed, it can start to create walls and distance between us. Once the emotional resentment walls get taller and stronger over time, it gets more and more difficult to connect. Once resentment builds to a certain level, the wall might become indestructible. This is where a lot of couples find themselves in a really tough situation. They view the marriage and the relationship as something that is now a burden and perhaps something they don't even want to be a part of anymore. We all know couples in this situation. As you read this book, you might be on your way to this situation unfolding in your life. If you get the sense that this is where things are headed, you have the power the to address it and get it back on the right path.

At the end of the day, the partnership aspect of our marriage isn't the sexy stuff. However, it's critical to get it right. Imagine if you worked in your current job but there was zero job description for what you actually did on a daily basis. On the flip side, if you are business owner, imagine you hired someone for a position, but you didn't give them any roles or responsibilities. They were simply left to figure out your business, what role they played, and how to best serve. We don't operate this way in other areas of our lives, so why should we expect that our marriage should be any different?

Roles

When it comes to our marriages, we each have gifts and strengths as individuals within the marital unit. Some of us are great at numbers and finances. Many of us enjoy door outdoor duties like lawn maintenance, gardening, etc. Some of us enjoy cooking while others enjoy the therapeutic effect of cleaning and decluttering. Perhaps one or both of us enjoys being the bread winner/s. Some of us enjoy doing laundry while others don't.

When Jess and I got married in 2003, we didn't have these roles identified. It created a lot of tension in our relationship because not only did we not know what our jobs were, but we also didn't enjoy the roles we were playing.

For example, when we first got married, I was in charge of the family finances (cashflow, bills, and budget). I was also in charge of the investing. I loved the investing aspect because I loved learning about stocks, mutual funds, IRAs, 401Ks, and different elements of investing for our future. I loved learning about companies in the public sector and investing in solid companies. I loved watching our money grow and I didn't really mind the short-term losses and pullbacks. Losing a few thousand dollars in the market didn't impact me that much. I knew it was just the flow of the market and losses were bound to happen.

On the flip side, I despised doing our monthly bills and budget. I hated seeing money go out the door for absolutely anything. It didn't matter if it was a vacation or paying our mortgage; I hated seeing money go out. When I would pull up our bank account and bill pay every week, I felt a sense of absolute dread. I also felt stressed when I was done paying bills. Doing the monthly budget and cash flow felt absolutely draining to me. Plus, if I am being honest, I wasn't the best at it. I jumped on the Dave Ramsey debt snowball early; right when we got married. Reason being, Jessica and I had substantial student loan debt ($64K combined) along with a new car payment of $385 per month ($25K new car when we got married). I was overwhelmed by the fact we had nearly $100K in debt and that wasn't including the home we'd just bought for $175K with a massive 7.25% interest rate. I felt I had to act fast, and I jumped into Financial Peace University right out of the gate. I did the bills for the first five years of our marriage and managed to pay off the student debt and our car within those first five years. However, I did it very recklessly.

I was so driven to get out of debt from an emotional standpoint. I literally threw every dollar and every cent we had at that debt. Sometimes only leaving us with twelve dollars in the bank account at a time. While I thought I was doing us a favor, I was actually driving Jessica into a frenzy because she was terrified when our account would get too low.

Looking back, I now understand why I was so driven from an emotional standpoint. Growing up, we didn't have a lot of money. My mom was in and out of jobs. I remember times in my childhood when she didn't even know how to make the next house payment or how she relentlessly cut coupons so we could have enough food for the week. I remember the emotional toll that took on both of us and I was determined not to have that stress in my adult life. However, I took it too far. I wasn't communicating what I was doing with our money with Jessica. I just took action. I was driven by my emotions of scarcity and not logic. Plus, I was fulfilling a role that was draining me and I wasn't good at it. While my intentions were good and we paid off 90K in debt, the journey was terrible for both of us.

After five long years of me doing the bills, Jessica came to me and said, "Why don't you let me take over the bills?"

At first, I was puzzled as to why she wanted to do this. My perception was that she wouldn't want to or it would stress her out. She told me, "Doing the bills doesn't stress me out. I have no emotional ties to seeing money go out. Plus, I am good at thinking about things we need or want several months out. I am frugal and I naturally do well with money. You, on the other hand, are an extreme mess when it comes to our bills. While you have paid off a lot of debt, it has also put a lot of tension on our relationship. Let me take over for a few months, and let's see how it goes. Plus, that will give you more time to invest our money right and to bring home more revenue for the family."

After a few months, we both learned it was the best decision. As a result, me handing over the budget and bills freed up my mental and emotional bandwidth to go out and earn more. Plus, our investments did a lot better because I was so focused on putting more time and energy into that.

Here we are, 15 years later, and it has been the best decision we have made for our financial peace. We have other roles as well. When she cooks, I clean up, and vice versa. When I give the boys a bath, she helps them brush their teeth, and vice versa. I do the lawn care, and she does a lot of the inside cleaning. She does laundry, and I do the folding. Obviously, our boys have their roles as well within the family unit.

The bottom line is this: we are both fulfilling our roles and living up to each other's expectations. Plus, we are doing the roles that are fulfilling to us and not draining us.

Most couples will simply assume a role is theirs or their spouse's. When expectations aren't met (even silent expectations) or we feel like roles aren't balanced, we get resentful and build emotional walls. This is truly unfortunate because it is something that can be easily avoided if only simply talked about and identified.

So, here is your to-do: take some time and make a list of every household duty and role. Then, communicate which roles you and your spouse like and which ones feel absolutely draining. Identify who does what and when. Then, go execute. Sounds simple, doesn't it? It is simple but it's not easy.

If it were easy, wouldn't most married couples do this? These aren't the sexy conversations to have; however, they are critical. If you don't want build emotional resentment, you need to get this ironed out.

Finances

This is an element in your marital partnership that you absolutely need to get clear on. Reason being is financial stress will absolutely end your marriage if you aren't clear on it.

As I mentioned before, over half of all divorces in the US are due to financial stress, arguments, and debt burden. There are several different financial personalities. Some people are savers and frugal while others are spenders. Some people are more like ostriches; they bury their head in the sand, never paying attention to what is happening with their money, and they hope everything will be OK.

This is another reason why getting clear on your values is so important, both your individual values and the values you share as a couple. When we know our values, we can make financial decisions as a couple that are in line with our marital/family vision. Not to mention, most women have a deep need for financial certainty. Married couples have to be aligned to the big picture and the micro decisions of the day to day. A weekly financial meeting (while sometimes isn't the most fun) is absolutely critical.

Jessica and I have been in perfect alignment with our financial vision for the better part of our marriage, but this wasn't always so. We used to argue about money, bills, and savings all the time. We also used to try and keep up with the Jones' with clothes, cars, even our home back in the day, which caused a ton of stress and pressure. We would buy nice things expecting happiness. The problem was the more money we spent, the less happy we found ourselves.

It wasn't until we got clear on our values that we finally understood where our money should go and why.

One of Jessica's core values is "environment." She loves being in a home that feels warm and inviting. She loves being in a home that brings her serenity. While that isn't at the very top of my core values, I will say it's way up there! We also found out we don't value status symbols like designer clothes or cars. We thought we did at one time, but we have realized through trial and error that we don't at all. We both value health and vitality, so it makes sense to us to spend more money on high quality healthy foods for us and the family. We both value "connection" with our family, so we are willing to spend money on experiences that create memories. In fact, one the mottos we live by in our family is "Experiences over stuff!" Every year for Christmas we spend no more than $50 to $100 on each of the boys. While that sounds insanely low for most families, we feel great about it. We take a decent amount of money and plan experiences with the boys for the following year.

Parenting

Next to finances, parenting is the element that couples fight about most. It's absolutely critical to get on the same page with values, operations, and discipline. If you don't go through this process, you are asking for resentment and tension.

When we first got married, we made every parenting mistake possible. She would punish harshly for things she felt strongly about, and I would do the same. However, the things we felt strongly about weren't always aligned. We would argue about discipline in front of the kids. If I disciplined a certain way and she didn't agree, she would argue my judgement in front of them. I would do the same. As a result, the kids knew we were misaligned, and they would work one of us against the other. We agreed on certain aspects of education and religion but not all. Overall, it was really messy.

After seeing a counselor early on in our marriage, we finally got alignment on this. We agreed on several things including no spanking and no disagreeing with the other in front of the kids. If one of us made a disciplinary call that the other didn't agree with, we would have that discussion in private and not in front of the kids. We came to an agreement on religion and how we would spiritually raise our kids. We agreed upon what type of education we would provide for the kids. We also agreed on unacceptable behavior from the kids like lying, cheating, stealing, and cursing. We had to get extremely clear on several other things as the boys got older like friends, sports, and even girlfriends.

The bottom line is this, get clear on how you parent the kids. Be on the same page. If you aren't on the same page, work together to agree on the middle-ground compromise.

When it comes to parenting, no one is perfect. However, its critical to get the big things right. Character, honor, integrity, faith, and honesty are always at the top. Kids will be kids, and they will make mistakes. They will forget to clean their room. Boys will pee all over the bathroom and toilet seat.

The Chores and Schedules

Running a household schedule can be extremely overwhelming, even with just two kids. Add three, four, five, and even more kids, and it can feel like a train that never stops. The calendar is full of extracurricular events and practices. The homework can feel like it never ends.

When it comes to chores, all six of us have our individual chores. We rotate the chores so the boys get a variety of duties. Jessica and I have ours as well. Everyone is responsible for their own laundry, even our boys. If something isn't clean that they want to wear, it's on them to clean it, wear it dirty, or wear something else. It's no one else's fault and there's no one to blame if their clothes aren't clean. It's their job, and they own it. The same goes for everyone's room. Everyone is in charge of keeping their rooms and spaces clean. It doesn't have to be clean or perfect 24/7, but once a week, each room gets picked up and cleaned. Everyone pitches in for prepping dinner, setting the kitchen table, and clean up.

When it comes to schedules for six people, documentation, communication, and ownership is a must. It's a common occurrence at least once or twice a week that Jessica and I have to divide and conquer getting the boys to school, activities, and events. We share a digital calendar and we all have a large dry erase board family calendar that everyone can consult. We know exactly what is coming up each day, week, and month for all of us. We communicate daily about who will do what and who is responsible. It might sound extreme, but our system avoids so many missteps, miscommunications, and arguments.

Everyone knows their jobs. Everyone knows their roles. Everyone knows their schedules and everyone else's. Our system might not be the best for you, but it works for us. I encourage you to find something that works for your unique situation.

Element #3: Friendship

One aspect of our marriages a lot of us overlook is the friendship aspect. The foundation of our relationship with our wives. The element that moves us from friends to lovers is the intimacy, sex, and flirting. A lot of us forget the fact we are friends at the very core. Over time, many of us give our friendships outside of our marriages more TLC than the friendship with our wives (and the same can be said for her). We tend to get distracted with the roles, chores, parenting, work, and the busyness, and if we don't pay attention, our friendship can drift over time. Many of us will actually give our coworkers more intention and attention during an interaction than we do with each other.

When we first get together and are dating each other, we are 150% intentional in the moment. We can't wait to talk to each other. We can't wait to hang out with each other. We do fun activities together and maybe even try new things that we otherwise wouldn't because we are in a relationship with someone new. Over time, we tend to get a little lazy and let things slide. When life gets crazy and things get busy, we tend to spend less time doing things together that elevate the relationship. Over time, our marriages can seem routine or even boring.

The bottom line is this...if we constantly treat each other like we did when we first started in the relationship, we can keep things fresh and passionate (even in the friendship aspect).

Be Intentional, Even When It's the Small Stuff

Back in 2015, I worked in corporate America in the medical device field. I had some pretty amazing coworkers and one of the best managers I had ever worked for. I always noticed that during company meetings, everyone was alert and on point. No one was distracted on their phones. When someone on our team spoke, others listened. We did a lot of team-building activities together like golf, indoor rock climbing, bowling, even things like escape rooms. When someone asked a question of the team or even our amazing manager, everyone listened, and no one talked. After questions were heard, people reflected back and gave suggestions intentionally. It was a pivotal time in my career when our entire team morale was an all-time high. Not only did we all work together, but we were also friends outside of work.

One day during a meeting, my manager was talking about his home life and the amazing relationship he had with his wife. He specifically talked about how they listened to each other when they spoke. They would put their phones down. They would mute the TV (or turn it off). In car rides they would turn off the radio when the other person wanted to talk. He also mentioned that they were always trying new things like axe throwing, ballroom dancing, playing poker, top golf, cooking classes, and even ice skating. What I noticed about the entire room is that everyone was shocked to hear how much effort he and his wife had put into their friendship over the 22 years they had been married. There were always new adventures and dates. It was an atmosphere of fun, adventure, and laughter. Both of them felt seen and heard over the years, and most importantly, they played by the same rules.

After everyone was complimenting how he went about his marriage and raving about he and his wife's practices and tactics, he made a point I will never forget.

He asked, "Have you guys ever noticed the amazing team morale we have here between all of us?"

We all looked at each other, and just by how we looked at each other, we all knew we felt the same way. Our team was connected. We made memories together. We played by rules like listening intently to each other. We appreciated each other. We knew the names of everyone's spouses and kids (even what activities they did). Everyone felt seen, heard, and valued. We all made memories with each other because we did new and fun team-building exercises with each other.

He went on to ask us, "Guys, can you imagine what the relationship/friendship with your spouse would be like if you just went at it with the same intention we do here? We give each other the gift of feeling seen and heard. How many times do you put down your phone or mute the TV when your spouse is talking to you? How many of you are creating new adventures and doing things you don't normally do? What if you treated your spouses with the same intention we do within our team here? How would that elevate things at home? Most people are on their best behavior in the workplace and get lazy at home. What if you treated your husband or wife with the same respect and intention we do on this team?" It was like a bomb went off in the room! You could tell it hit home with all of us.

What would it be like to get even those small things right? When your wife speaks to you, do you put down your phone and look in her eyes? Does she do the same? Do you mute the TV (or turn it off) when you speak up or ask something? Do you take time do go out and do new things to create new experiences?

Bottom line is this...give each other the gift of feeling seen and heard. Hang on her every word. She should hang on your every word, too. Go out and do things you otherwise wouldn't to create new connections and experiences. Sound too good to be true or even too hard? Well, there is an alternative...keep drifting and don't cultivate the friendship our marriages are based on.

Get into Each Other's Worlds

One of the things that can put a wedge in our marriages is having completely separate interests. Let's get straight on one thing: we won't ever have all the same interests, and that is completely fine. We should have individual interests. However, we can intentionally decide to take interest in our spouse's interest and see the world through their eyes with them.

It's not the easiest thing in the world to go check out a painting class with her because she loves to paint if you don't. However, it would most likely mean the world to her if you painted with her and did something with her that made her come alive.

She may not like baseball, and maybe you're a season ticket holder. It might be pretty awesome if she went to a few games with you because she knew how much you enjoyed it and wanted to spend that time with you.

For you it might not be painting and baseball. Perhaps it's other things. At the end of the day, get into each other's worlds and interests. No one says you suddenly have to become Picasso and she learns every player's stats on your favorite team. It's simply a gesture of being giving with your time and genuinely interested in what brings the other person to life.

Bottom line is this...get curious about each other's worlds and get involved with each other's interests. You can make it an adventure. You can make it memorable. It doesn't have to be perfect. In fact, this gives each of you a great excuse to be imperfect students of each other.

Being Her Friend Doesn't Mean Fixing Her Problems

When men are in distress, we usually do one of two things. We either isolate or we go to a trusted friend for support, guidance, and advice. Let's be honest here—men have to really be in a desperate situation to do the latter most of the time. And honestly, that's really unfortunate. Every man needs trusted advisors when life gets crazy, but we will tackle that later. For now, let's get back to you and her.

Being her friend means you listen, create space, and emotionally validate what she is feeling—not fix her problems. I know this totally goes against what you think you need to do. I've been doing this work for years and I still have to stop myself from doing it to my wife to this day. Men have different needs than women do when it comes to fixing problems and giving advice. When a man asks another man what to do in a time of crisis, he is looking for guidance. He wants ideas on making his situation better.

Women (in general, not all) are different. They don't necessarily want advice. They don't want us to fix it. They don't want us "shoulding" all over them. If don't know what that means, it means we usually like to say things like:

"You should make the kids pack their own lunches so you don't always feel the need to do it yourself."

"You should tell your friend how you feel and make sure she knows where you stand!"

"You should tell your mom and dad that you are sick and tired of them butting into our life."

At times, we can take massive, heaping, steaming piles of "SHOULD" on our wives. Truth be told, most of the time, that isn't what they want. In order to strengthen the friendship and relationship, all we really need to do is listen, create some space, and emotionally validate where they are at.

Men and women are wired a bit different when it comes to this. There are actually a few books out there for men that address the dynamic like *Men Are from Mars, Women Are from Venus* by John Grey and *Way of the Superior Man* by David Deida. It boils down to the fact that when men communicate, our main objective is to share ideas, problem solve, and share opinions. Women are a bit different. They communicate to simply elevate the bond between us. So when a woman simply talks, she can feel dismissed, not heard, or even condescended when we bombard them with new ideas and opinions to "help them." I realize to you, being a guy like me, that this seems completely counterintuitive. Not to mention, we think we are doing the women in our lives a massive disservice by not offering our problem-solving advice. Take it from a man who not only helps men with this very tactic but also as one who understands because there are times I still have to stop myself from doing it myself.

If you want to strengthen the friendship aspect with your wife, you have to be willing to simply listen. Just creating space and using empathy are very powerful tools.

One of the best experts on the topic of empathy is Chris Voss (bestselling author of *Never Split the Difference* and former Chief Hostage Negotiator for the FBI). Chris calls intentional empathy in action tactical empathy. Tactical empathy is the skill of making the person you are talking to feel seen, heard, and even understood. Tactical empathy doesn't require agreement. Let me say that again: tactical empathy doesn't require agreement. We can let other people know that we see and hear them, but it doesn't mean that we agree. How people are operating, what they are doing, and even how they see the world makes total sense to them. Chris uses several examples in his book *Never Split the Difference* of how some of the terrorists he had to negotiate with he didn't agree with at all. At times, he was negotiating with extremists who were threatening to end the lives of innocent people because of their religious beliefs. Chris explains that while we don't agree with killing innocent people because our religious beliefs, to some people, killing in the name of religion makes total sense.

The same goes for our wives. She might be operating in a way that seems odd or even crazy to you, but it makes total sense to her. She might be overwhelmed and feel underappreciated due to the mess the kids leave behind. She feels angry that she is doing all the heavy lifting of the housework and she feels no one is helping. When the women in our lives articulate feelings like this, we automatically feel the need to do several different things.

1. We can defend ourselves against a personal attack that we feel she might be making on us directly.

2. We can immediately start problem solving the issue and create new rules that the entire family now has to live by.

3. We can do one of the worst things and ask: "Why are you so upset about this? This isn't a big deal!"

Again, tactical empathy doesn't mean agreement. It simply means you are validating what she is feeling in that moment. When we validate and use empathy, she is more likely to feel seen and heard.

When she feels that from you, she will ultimately feel more connected to you as a friend and lover.

The most important part of this is the "how." How do we use tactical empathy? Chris Voss goes on to explain that we can use a variety of responses, and they all have a similar theme.

When our wives come at us with problems or issues (like the one above), we can respond with:

"Sounds like…"

"Looks like…"

"Feels like…"

"Seems like…"

Here is a response I would use based on the situation above.

"Sounds like you are feeling underappreciated and even angry that you feel like you are doing a lot of the cleaning around here. How can I best support you right now? What feels right?"

What I just did in that moment, is I validated what my wife felt. I used the words "underappreciated" and "angry." I didn't say the phrases "What I am hearing you say…" or "What I am seeing here is…" because then it becomes all about me and not her feelings. Also, notice there was nothing in my response that stated I agreed with her. Maybe I do and maybe I don't, but for now I just want her to be validated.

By asking the questions "How can I best support you right now?" and "What feels right?", I am asking her to reflect on what help would be best for her in that moment. Notice I am also using the words "what feels right" because I want to validate her feelings, but I can also encourage her to think logically.

She might respond with several different things.

She might say: "I just need to vent for a minute."

She also might say: "I really want to think of a way we divide up the household duties."

It doesn't really matter. Most likely she will tell you exactly what she needs in that moment.

In order to optimize the friendship aspect of our marriages, we have to really utilize this powerful and critical communication skill. If we don't, we will always come back to the same result of her talking, you problem solving, her being frustrated because you aren't listening, her feeling unheard, and you wondering why she doesn't understand your advice. More on this topic later.

Element #4: Lovers

This might be the favorite section of the book for the majority of the readers. This is where we cover sex.

What might shock you is that this element will be the shortest read compared to the first three elements. There is a reason for that.

Men are sexual creatures by nature. For the most part, we receive love and give love in a physical way. It's usually during sex we feel most loved and accepted. Sex is a huge part of our marriage. It is literally the biggest difference that separates couples from the friend zone.

In order for us to optimize our sex lives, it's critical the other three elements are firing on all cylinders. Most of us like to skip over one, two, or even all three of the previous elements and get straight to the lovers element. It's no secret that men can turn on and off the sexual aspect of our relationship pretty easily. For women, it's not the same. Women need a great deal of connection outside of the bedroom in order for it to be an elevated experience in the bedroom.

In order to really understand this, we have to keep in mind the needs of both men and women. When we understand the needs of both and we fulfill both, that's when our relationships feel like they are on fire. Both men and women have three basic needs.

Women need to feel seen, heard, and safe.

Men need to feel respected, appreciated, and validated.

For a woman, to be seen is to be appreciated and loved. For a woman, to be heard is to be loved and appreciated. Some of us, by nature, aren't the best at observation. Some of us aren't the best at listening. Some of us are good at observation and/or listening. For the most part, it doesn't really matter if we are good at observation or listening because it simply needs to be spoken and communicated to our wives that we see them and hear them.

Many of our wives are constantly doing things for the family. By nature they juggle a lot of things. To really hit this home, I will share some examples from my own marriage.

Jessica and I have four crazy boys. She is the only female in the house. She jokes all the time that she is surrounded by 10 balls, a ton of energy, dishes, laundry, and absolute mayhem from time to time. For a woman who needs to be seen and heard, it can be a complex situation to get her needs met.

I run a massive platform to help men live legendary lives, cultivate legendary connections under their own roofs, and create the extraordinary marriage of their dreams. If I allowed it, I could easily work 23 hours per day and still not get everything done. My boys require a lot of time and energy. My self-care requires my time and energy. My coaching clients and men in our mastermind require a lot of my time and energy. Luckily, doing this work has allowed me to learn and teach the skills to optimize my marriage.

My job as a husband is to fulfill Jessica's three basic needs in the best way possible. To be honest, for someone who doesn't know how to do that (most of us miss the mark on this), it can feel complex and even overwhelming. We tend to overthink it. We don't have to do that. It's actually easier than we think.

Every single day, I make an intentional effort and promise to myself to SEE her. Not just see her but acknowledge and appreciate something I saw her do. For example, as I sit here and write this very paragraph, she texted me asking me if I needed anything from the grocery store. One of her jobs that she owns is grocery shopping. I go sometimes, but she pretty much owns that job. Being real here, grocery shopping for six people, five of them males, isn't for the faint of heart. As quickly as the pantry gets filled, it gets emptied. To her grocery shopping is not a fun experience. She actually somewhat despises it. When I am done writing today, my plan is to go up to her and tell her how much I appreciate her for shopping for our family. When I share that acknowledgement, I do it with intention.

I will make sure my boys are in the room when I acknowledge her. Acknowledging our wives publicly and in front of our kids is extremely impactful. Not only do they feel seen and appreciated, but they feel publicly seen and appreciated. When we are publicly appreciated, it elevates the entire experience of being appreciated. We feel more seen. We feel more appreciated. Plus, if my boys see me publicly appreciate my wife, they will always do the same. It also teaches them a valuable lesson on how they can appreciate the women in their lives when they get older.

Here is what I will say in front of the boys: "Babe, thank you so much for going to the grocery store today! I know it isn't your favorite thing to do. I honestly don't know what we would do without you. Not only do you shop for the family, but you are always so considerate to get specific things that you know each one of us really likes. Love you and appreciate you." Not only will I say that very thing, but I will hold her hands and look her square in the eyes with a loving voice tone. It sounds so simple, and quite frankly, it is. All we really have to do to acknowledge and appreciate our wives is see something they do specifically and acknowledge it with intention.

A woman also needs to feel heard to feel love and appreciation. I'm going to throw myself on the sword and admit I am a work in progress on this one. Jessica's number-one complaint is that sometimes I don't listen very well. Full transparency, I don't listen well all the time. My house is loud with a lot of energy, and at times, it's hard to focus. At times, I am distracted and on my phone too much while she is talking to me. I don't get on my phone while she is talking to me, but at times, she begins a conversation with me while I am doing something on my phone and I don't pay attention immediately. At times, I can be in my head and distracted with what feels like hundreds of demands. To be honest, it doesn't matter what the situation or excuse is, my wife needs know her voice matters. Nothing makes her feel more unimportant than not being heard.

In order to ensure I am listening, I need to implement certain tactics that sound very simple, yet they can get missed from time to time.

First, if she is talking, I physically put my phone away and out of sight. Simon Sinek teaches this very tactic. He shares that people report feeling disconnected from a conversation with someone who has a phone in their hand. So, get clear on that. We don't even have to be on our phones for someone to feel disconnected from us. Just having it in in our hands or in sight will send the signal that we aren't as connected as we might intend to be.

Secondly, I reflect back what she has told me so she knows I heard her. There are ways to optimize reflecting back to someone that ensure they feel seen and heard. We have all been in conversations with someone and felt they weren't even listening even though they were quiet and looking at us when we were speaking. Reflecting back to someone optimally is a skill. One of the most basic ways to reflect back to someone involves using tactical empathy, as described in the previous section.

We can also use a skill set called mirroring. Mirroring is literally just repeating the last three words someone said to us or three key words they said to us. When we mirror the last three words or key words someone has stated, it sends a signal that we heard them because we are using their words. Psychologically, it also invites them to tell you more information or to go on with their thought or story. People by nature feel good when they are invited to share more. Another important tip when it comes to mirroring is that we should steer clear of using the word "why." When we use the word "why," it can feel unsafe and condescending. It can also put the other person on the defense if not used in the right tone of voice.

Here is a real-world example of what NOT to do and why.

There have been many days I have come home to find the house a total mess. The kids are loud. There is stuff everywhere. I can see by the look on Jessica's face that it might have been one of those days where everything and everyone has challenged her.

When I ask how her day is going, she might say, "Today was horrible! The kids trashed the whole house and are driving me crazy!"

My response when I didn't know what I was doing was something along the lines of: "Why are the kids driving you crazy? What happened? Why are you so angry?"

Here's why you don't respond like this.

When she is in this heightened emotional state, what she really needs is to be heard and seen. When I jump right in with the "why" question, even though I mean well because I really want to know, it doesn't land well. The word "why" can be taken as condescending, which puts people on the defensive. It literally puts us back to our experiences as a kid, when our parents would say something like: "Why did you do that? Why are you crying? Why can't you (fill in the blank)?"

Using the word WHY in a context like this will not only make someone feel inferior and somewhat defensive, but also the level of psychological safety has been lowered because to some degree they might feel wrong for having those feelings or even a bad moment.

Instead, use mirroring.

Take the same situation.

There have been many days when I have come home to find the house a total mess. The kids are loud. There is stuff everywhere. I can see by the look on Jessica's face that it might have been one of those days where everything and everyone has challenged her.

When I ask how her day is, she might say: "Today was horrible! The kids trashed the whole house and are driving me crazy!"

Mirroring response: "The kids are driving you crazy?" What is most important is I will ensure that my voice will inflect up with curiosity. I absolutely will not use a tone that sounds judgmental or condescending. When we use the other person's words and in the right tone, it invites them in to tell you more without using the word "why." By using their words, they feel heard. The other person will naturally tell you more information. Mirroring will also elevate the environment of psychological safety. When people feel seen and heard with the right tone of voice that is inviting, they naturally feel safe and more connected.

At this point, you are probably wondering why I haven't covered the topic of how to improve the sexual connection with your wife or even the frequency. To be honest, there is no need to do that because if you are fulfilling her three basic needs and optimizing the three other elements, sex and a lot of it is a natural result. Couples naturally have better sex more often when the relationship is truly elevated in the three elements and the three basic needs are being met.

8 DATE HER

"Do what you did in the beginning of the relationship and there won't be an end."

— Anthony Robbins

When it comes to creating an extraordinary marriage, there are several things that must become the norm. One of the most important aspects of creating an extraordinary marriage is dating our wives. Taking our wives out on dates are one of the most effective activities that we can incorporate into our weekly routine—and it truly is low-hanging fruit. If you can't take your wife out weekly, then biweekly is the bare minimum.

I've been doing work with men/husbands/fathers since 2011. Over the past several years, I have listened to what is on the minds and hearts of men as it relates to their marriages. I have been honored to hear well over two thousand stories over the past decade. I have heard stories of ultimate marriage success and stories of absolute disaster. What I can tell you is I have learned what works from other successful couples what works. I have also learned what doesn't work through couples that struggle. I have also had to learn many of these lessons firsthand in my own marriage over the past 20 years.

What I can tell you, without any doubt, is that the couples that flourish and elevate their relationship are the ones who continue to date and court each other. They take deliberate time every week (or at least every two weeks) to go out on a date with each other. Successful couples experience the benefits of being away from the home and kids on a regular basis where they don't have to be Mom and Dad. When we briefly break away from being our parental roles, from the busyness of life, and from the demands of our schedules, we can elevate the connection in our marriages.

Couples that take time to date each other on a regular basis report benefits such as: more intimacy, improved communication, higher frequency of sex, more passion for the relationship, and more fun and zest in the relationship and even in the family as a whole. When married couples are more fulfilled and happier, our kids will reap the benefits of that as well.

One of the challenges I hear most is many of us think we don't have the time to date our wives. After all, between work, kids' activities, their schoolwork, and the overall busyness of the family, dating can seem a little superfluous and challenging to try and fit into our schedules. What I can tell you from my own experience and the experiences of countless other men is that we don't have time not to. Even if we have to dial back on some of the other activities, it's worth it! Life (and married life) is just too short to go through it not feeling connected to the woman we love on the highest level.

Another challenge that is brought up frequently is that we have no idea what we would talk about on our date nights, even if we had them. After all, if we have been married 5, 10, 15, 20-plus years, don't we know everything about each other anyway? The answer to that is NO! As human beings, we are always evolving, changing, and growing. To some extent there are some things that don't change about us, but overall, we do change. Think about it for a moment. If you are in your 30s, are you the exact same person you were in your 20s? If you are in your 40s, are you the same person you were in your 30s? The answer is NO! We change. We grow. We evolve. When it comes to dating each other in our marriages, it's critical to stay curious about each other and constantly get to know each other over and over again. Keeping love alive in a marriage is about falling in love with the same person for all the years to come.

I've known Jessica for the past 25 years, and we have been married for 20. For the first half of our marriage, we didn't go out as a couple very much. We were busy raising our boys when they were little at the time. When we did go out, we usually went out with our own friends separately. I would go out with my guy friends for "guy's night out" and Jessica would go out for "girl's night out." Jessica and I barely spent time with each other outside the home and even away from the boys. We always thought that since we saw each other every day, that was enough. After all, we were raising our young boys together, so wasn't that enough time spent together? The answer was (and still is) a hard "NO." In the beginning, our marriage paid for that. We weren't nearly as close as we are now. Our sex life wasn't the best when we weren't taking time to date each other. Our communication definitely wasn't on point because we weren't taking time to connect with each other outside of being parents. The relationship often felt like we were spinning in different orbits. We were still together, but not really aligned. As a result, the stress in the marriage felt heavy and somewhat disengaged. This resulted in feelings of disconnection, needs not being met, and the beginning stages of resentment. When we started implementing a weekly/biweekly date night, our foundation was renewed, and our connection was reinvigorated. We felt more aligned and connected. Our passion for each other and our marriage came back. Our intimacy and sex life became more frequent and more exciting. As a result of being more fulfilled in our marriage, our boys began to see their mom and dad as more patient, more fulfilled, and happier overall.

One of the biggest lessons I have learned from this mission is that we (parents) are the foundation of the house that our family is built on. We wouldn't think about building a home on an unstable or broken foundation. The foundation would eventually become so weak that it could no longer withstand the task of holding up the house. As a result, the house would fall and crumble. The family is no different. We (parents) are the foundation of our families. Our kids will derive strength from the foundation we provide as parents. Couples (parents) who take time to constantly strengthen the foundations of their marriages will provide a stronger foundation for the entire family. Many of us think it's selfish to take time away from our kids to strengthen the marriage, but it's not selfish at all. Our kids will benefit from seeing their parents thrive and not just survive. Keep in mind, our kids have a front-row seat to either a functional or dysfunctional marriage. Boys will learn how to love their girlfriends and eventually wives by the example we set for them as their father. Girls will learn how to be loved by how we love their mom. Think of it this way; we have an amazing opportunity to show our kids how we can purposely and intentionally love our spouses.

9 LISTEN FOR FEELINGS, NOT JUST WORDS

"Be a good listener... It makes the other person who's speaking to you feel loved, cared for, and worthy of being heard."

— Wayne Dyer

In Element #3 of an extraordinary marriage, I briefly described the skill of tactical empathy. Most of us miss the mark completely when it comes to connecting with our wives when they come to us to talk or even vent.

I remember early in my marriage to Jessica that I loved when she would come and talk to me about things. I especially loved when she would come vent to be about a situation that was overwhelming to her and she didn't know exactly what to do. She would come to me with a range of issues and topics! Sometimes she would come talk to me about situations at work. Other times it was things she was dealing with that were mom related. Other times, it could be simply a random situation that was bringing up feelings of stress or overwhelm. I enjoyed it because I love helping people solve problems. I also really enjoyed being the guy that could provide an environment where we could logically talk through complex issues that would result in a solution.

In years past, I would get frustrated or even somewhat deflated when Jess would come to be with a problem, I would give her advice, and it was met with "You aren't hearing me" or "You aren't really listening to me." I remember being so frustrated and confused when she would come to me with a clear issue, and I helped come up with a very clear potential solution. There were even times in our relationship when I would get angry because I felt she wasn't hearing my "words of wisdom." After all, wasn't that the reasons she was coming to me and venting to me in the first place?

Even as I type out the words above, I have a smile on my face, knowing that I was missing what she really needed. What she really needed was to be heard, supported, and validated. I had to learn the hard way that when our wives come to us with things that are challenging them, what they are really wanting is connection, safety, and love. They don't necessarily want a solution. At times, they want potential solutions, but most of the time connection, safety, and love are key.

It can be a very confusing thing for us men because we are wired to problem solve. In fact, that is how we show love and support. We want to provide solutions that take away pain. We want to contribute to the solution of a problem because we love her and don't want to see her in pain. So, it makes total sense for us to listen and then offer up advice. Not to mention, when we don't do this, we can feel absolutely useless.

When it comes to really listening to our wives, it's actually most effective to be empathetic and validate her feelings. We don't even need to worry about a potential solution or advice most of the time because that's not what is needed. All we really have to do is focus on what she is feeling and label that emotion (anger, overwhelm, joy, excitement, frustration, etc.). It seems almost too simple. It actually feels so simple that we think it's most likely ineffective. But it's incredibly effective, again, because our wives are talking to us because they want to be seen, heard, loved, and validated. We actually do the opposite when we try and solve every problem that comes their way.

There is a video on YouTube called "It's Not About the Nail" that is an absolute classic. In all honesty, it's hysterical. If you have never seen the video, go take two minutes and watch it. After seeing it, you will get it. In fact, you might just feel like Neo from *The Matrix* after he took the red pill!

The video shows a young couple sitting on a couch, face to face. From the camera angle, you can't really see the woman's face for the first 20 seconds or so, but you can hear her explaining to her husband how much pain she is feeling in her head. She goes into detail about the nagging, throbbing pain between her eyes and says that no matter what she does, the pain will not go away. As the man listens intently, he also looks very confused and almost aggravated with the conversation the more she describes what she is feeling. After about 20 seconds, viewers can now fully see the woman's face to reveal that she has a large nail sticking out of her forehead. When it's revealed to the viewer that this nail is obviously causing all the issues, the video becomes hysterical. The man who is listening to her looks frustrated and completely confused as to why she is complaining about all the pain she is feeling. After listening to her for 30 to 40 painful seconds, he finally states the obvious: "Well, you know, you do have a large nail sticking right out of the front of your head!"

She fires back, offended, and says, "It is not about the nail! You always do this! You never listen. All you want to do is solve a problem, and all I really want you do to is listen."

The man looks totally confused and offended that his wife isn't hearing him and simply taking his advice to pull out the nail. After bickering back and forth, he finally agrees to not give advice and just listen. As she goes on longer about the pain and frustration of dealing with the nail in her head, he responds by validating her feelings instead of solving the problem by saying, "That sounds really hard." With a sigh of relief, his wife holds his hand and confirms that is exactly what she is feeling and thanks him for listening.

I've seen this video several times, and every time it makes me laugh. I find the humor in it because of its truth of the misunderstanding men and women feel when we communicate. Men want to solve problems and take away pain because we love our wives. Our wives will communicate problems and pain because they want connection, not solutions.

Again, I had to learn this the hard way early in my marriage. Men and women are wired different, and that is OK. The most important aspect of creating a solid foundation of communication is simply understanding the different needs of both sides and knowing what to do.

The next time your wife comes to you with a problem, an issue, a situation that is overwhelming, or if she is just looking to vent, listen to every word and help label the emotions she is feeling.

Sometimes the most effective response can be something like: "That sounds overwhelming. Who wouldn't be overwhelmed? How can I best support you? What feels right?" When we respond with an emotional label (overwhelming) we see her, hear her, and create an environment of safety. When we add "Who wouldn't be overwhelmed?", we are normalizing and validating what she is feeling in that moment. By normalizing the feeling, we are validating that emotion. When we validate the emotion, we are doubling down on the feeling of safety and connection. When we ask the questions, "How can I best support you?" and "What feels right?", we engage *her* thoughts and feelings in what we can do for her. I especially like to use the words "What *feels* right?" because in her vulnerable state, she is feeling more than thinking. She is sharing her emotions, not just her thoughts. Our wives are "feeling beings" with a lot of emotions. When we communicate with them in that way, it lands better for them and improves the connection overall.

So, when it comes to being a good listener, it's not just about the solving the problem or listening to just the words. It's about hearing her and identifying what she is feeling.

10 THE QUALITY OF YOUR RELATIONSHIP IS DETERMINED BY THE QUALITY OF YOUR QUESTIONS

> *"The quality of your life and your relationships are determined by the questions you ask of yourself and others."*
> — Mark Divine (retired Navy SEAL Commander)

"**H**ow was your day?" used to be my go-to question for everyone in my family when I would see them in the evenings. I would always get back similar one-word answers with very little depth or detail. I would hear "fine, good, busy, crazy, boring, not good, OK, etc." I found that getting these one-word answers would result in me not knowing exactly where to take the conversation. In fact, I would find it frustrating from time to time, wondering why I couldn't get better answers from Jessica or the boys.

Talking to most men, this is the daily go-to question we default to when we see our loved ones in the evening after a long day of school and work. Most of us get irritated over time that this question doesn't somehow open up an amazing conversation with connection and depth with our loved ones. All of us dream about a day where we come home from work and get into a deep discussion with our wives and kids around how they experienced life that day. The reason we ask questions in the first place is to create connection through good conversations. Deep conversations are the pathways to deep connections with our loved ones. I'm not just talking about shallow high-level conversations that are simply an exchange of information. We want the types of conversations where authenticity, vulnerability, and deep connection become the standard.

Back in 2018, I earned my second coaching certification in a discipline called Xchange, which is based on an approach called Appreciative Inquiry. Appreciative Inquiry was founded in 1987 by David Cooperrider and Suresh Srivastva and is commonly called an "asset-based" or "strengths-based" approach to systems change because it emphasizes positive idea generation over negative problem identification (or deficit-based approach). The model of AI uses questions and dialogue to help people uncover existing assets, strengths, advantages, or opportunities within individuals, communities, organizations, or teams and then collectively work toward developing and implementing strategies for improvement. This is a long way to say that Appreciative Inquiry provides a way to teach human beings to bring out the best of what was (the past), the best of the current (the present), and the best of what could be (the future). Most human beings operate with the mentality of negative problem identification and problem solving. We are constantly viewing the world through the lens of what is wrong and how we can fix it. The AI approach is much different. It trains us to find the strengths and assets from past, present, and future. When we approach situations, individuals, communities, organizations, and teams with this approach, we bring out the best.

So, what does this have to do with marriage and deepening our relationships? A lot actually.

When we ask high-quality, deep questions of our wives (and even kids), we are engaging them in storytelling about how they experienced the world that day. The most important thing is asking the right questions. To be honest, it really isn't that hard. It's a slight tweak to the ever-so-boring default question: "How was your day?"

Years ago, I started asking Jessica (and my kids) very different questions when I would see them in the evening. What I found was that asking better questions completely changed the entire dynamic of the conversation and connection. I found that when I asked better questions, she would come to life. She would light up and story tell about her day! When she lit up, so would I. When people are both lit up and connected during conversation, it adds more connection, depth, authenticity, vulnerability, and intimacy to the relationship.

So, instead of asking "How was your day?", I would ask a variety of the questions below:

1. What was the best part of your day, and why was it so meaningful?
2. What was something that made you smile today?
3. Share a moment with me today that made you laugh.
4. What is something you are proud of that happened today?
5. If you could relive a moment today, what would it be and why?
6. What was something you learned today, and can you teach it to me?
7. If you had to relive today, what is a moment you would love to relive twice?
8. What was something you were thankful for today?

Any one of these above questions will create a conversation with your wife. These are powerful questions because they invite her to pick a high-point moment of her day and tell a story about what happened. When two people share in a high-point moment story that is meaningful, it creates trust, depth, connection, and even intimacy. These high-quality questions will not only create connection every single day, but they will improve the relationship overall. And these are just the daily questions!

In The Dad Edge Alliance Mastermind community, we not only teach men about asking questions like this on a daily basis; we also teach how to reflect back what you hear and validate the feelings behind the stories. Remember, when we reflect back and validate feelings, we are fulfilling her three biggest needs: to feel seen, heard, and safe.

A common conversation with Jessica and I would look like this:

Me: "Hey, love. What was the best part of your day, and why was it so meaningful?"

Jessica (smiles and lights up): "I got to talk to my mom today! It has been about a month since we have gotten a chance to catch up. I told her all about the boys, their good grades, and the sports we are playing right now. I also told her about how I decorated the basement a couple of weeks ago. We decided to get together this weekend for a quick coffee. It was awesome talking to her."

Me (smiling and listening to every word): "That sounds amazing! I bet it was awesome catching up with her especially since it has been a while! Tell me what you are most looking forward to when you guys meet up on Saturday for coffee."

Jessica (still smiling and still lit up): "I'm just really excited to see her. I always feel like something is kind of missing in my life when I don't see or talk to her often. So, this will be really good for both of us!"

Me (still smiling): "I have no doubt! You always seem so recharged after you spend some time with her! That sounds amazing!"

The above was a real conversation. These are real conversations that happen every single day. Not every day is filled with sunshine, rainbows, and gratitude. Some days are met with challenge and things that weren't positive. That's OK. What we are looking to do here is create depth, authenticity, and intimacy. When we ask deeper questions where she is compelled to story tell and cannot answer the question with one word, the spark of connection has been ignited.

If you are finding it difficult to create connection with your wife out of thin air, I invite you to start asking her deeper questions that will spark connection and conversation. The same old simple default questions like "How was your day?" will never create the depth or connection in the relationship we truly desire. Make a promise to yourself and the people you love that you will never ask this default question again. It's a lazy question that requires little to no thought, and it will result in an answer that requires little to no thought.

Ask better questions. Reflect back and validate. Create connection and intimacy.

11 IT'S A WE, NOT YOU OR ME

> *"When it comes to marriage, many of us think that it's a me and you. It's actually WE, not me and you."*
> — Dr. Lee Baucom (founder of Save The Marriage)

I will never forget the time when we were vacationing in Florida in 2009. At the time, my oldest, Ethan, was three, and Mason was only eight months old. We were in our hotel room taking a break from the beach. We had come back to grab some lunch, take a break from the hot summer Florida sun, and change Mason's diaper. Everything about the trip was going so well. The boys (even though they were so little) were having so much fun on the beach. The weather was cooperating, and it was one of those trips where everything seemed to be perfect.

Before we left to go back to the beach, we needed to get Mason a fresh diaper. Jessica laid him on the bed to change him and reached for a new diaper that was sitting on the nearby nightstand. She didn't look away for more than about two seconds, but it was enough time that Mason had decided to start rolling over and over. Suddenly, before she could catch him, he had rolled right off the bed and onto the hard tile floor. Mason hit the floor hard and immediately started screaming in such a way that we knew he was really hurt. We both gasped and ran over to him on the floor. We picked him up and began to console him. However, he was so upset and so scared that it took several minutes to get him to calm down. Luckily, there was no permanent damage, but it could have been bad. Jessica immediately became emotional. She started blaming herself for not paying closer attention. She was overcome with so much guilt that she let her baby boy roll off the bed and hit the hard tile floor face first.

I tried to console her, hug her, and tell her it was OK, but she was extremely upset and racked with guilt. She ended up putting Mason in a baby backpack carrier and taking him for a walk on the beach. She insisted that she wanted to walk on the beach alone with him on her back and didn't want company. I found out later that she walked the beach for nearly an hour, sobbing and beating herself up with guilt. Truth be told, she wasn't changing Mason alone. I was right there with her. I too wasn't paying close enough attention. The truth of the matter is the situation also fell on my shoulders, not just hers. She felt the entire situation was all her fault and it could have been avoided if she was paying closer attention, but that wasn't the truth. We were both standing there, and we were in it together.

After she had gotten back from her walk on the beach with Mason and had calmed down, she came to me and apologized for what had happened. She was taking all the blame. After I consoled her, I told her it wasn't her fault alone. I was standing right there as well. I could have done something, but I too wasn't paying close enough attention. From that moment on, we decided our marriage was a WE, not a "me" or "you." We both brought our boys into this world, and they are our responsibility. If one of us screws up, we both screw up. If one of us succeeds, we both succeed. We are a team of WE, and we are better together.

We have viewed our marriage through the lens of WE ever since that day. There have been several times I have made mistakes that were fully my fault, but not once has Jessica allowed me to take full ownership. She shares in that ownership as well. Much like a football team is not made up of just one star player but eleven teammates all working together for the same goal! A successful quarterback cannot be successful without an effective offensive line. A successful quarterback cannot successfully execute a pass without an able receiver who can catch the ball.

The same is true for our marriages. We win together, we lose together, we celebrate together, we face the fire together, and we do life together. We are WE!

When it comes to our marriage, what would it look like to share in ownership like that? It's not easy, but it makes the journey of life so much more enjoyable.

12 LEAD HER

*"Show me a husband who leads well, and
I'll show you a wife who feels loved."*

— Ryan Fredrick

When Jessica and I got married, I wasn't the best at leading her. I used to have this skewed perspective of what it meant to lead Jessica. When it came to date nights, I always thought the polite thing to do was for her to make the decision on where we would go. I always thought the kind and thoughtful thing to do was to do whatever she wanted to do. I would also lean on her heavily to make decisions for the kids. What sports teams we would sign them up for. The activities they would be involved in. She made decisions on what we would eat for family dinners. She would make the decisions on the clothes they would wear and even toys we would buy them. I didn't mind her calling the shots on a lot of the above and would rarely even give my opinion. In fact, I thought that's what nice/thoughtful men did. After all, I love her and don't want to come across overbearing or demanding. What

I found out later in our marriage was that she hated making all the decisions and taking charge on so much. It actually felt heavy to her to make so many decisions on her own without input or opinion from me. I had no clue. What I thought was a thoughtful and unselfish approach was actually creating more stress for her.

I have been married to Jessica for the past 19 years and I found out in recent years that she actually hates making decisions on family dinners. She hates making the sole decision for six of us and she hates prepping dinner every day. Over the past few years, I've stepped up and taken charge on family dinners. I make the decisions on what we will have and take responsibility for prepping it. Once I started doing that, a sense of relief came over Jessica because she was no longer 100-percent responsible for making family dinner decisions on a nightly basis. In fact, she truly doesn't care what we have. She loves it when I say, "Hey, babe, on Tuesday, Thursday, and Saturday I've got dinner covered. No need to worry about getting what we need or prepping it. Just show up at 6:00 p.m. at the table. A sense of relief comes over her when decisions are simply taken off her plate (pun intended ☺).

Like I said above, I used to leave all date-night decisions and activities up to her (I still do sometimes, but not all). What I have found is that what she (as well as a lot of wives) appreciates most is simply a heads up around what time to be ready and some ideas around the dress code needed for what we will be doing. I take care of reservations for our meal, booking the activity, etc. I also take care of any childcare needs for the night and secure the babysitters. I'll simply tell Jessica, "Friday night, be ready by 6:00 p.m. Workout clothing is perfect for what we are going to do." Or I might say, "Friday night, be ready by 6:00 p.m. Wear something you don't mind getting paint on (if I'm taking her to a place like

Painting with a Twist). Your mom is already taking care of the kids for the night. They are spending the night at her house."

Being led like this is something my wife loves and craves, and over the past several years working with men (and couples), I have learned that most women, not just Jessica, truly want input, opinions, and more collaboration when it comes to making decisions. What a lot of us underestimate is the workload and the number of decisions our wives make on a daily basis. When women are overwhelmed by chores, tasks, to-do's, and decisions, it actually takes them out of their feminine energy and puts them more into their masculine energy. When women are more in their masculine and less in their feminine, they feel less sexy and more disconnected. When we take the lead like this, it feels better for them overall. They enjoy not being the one that is calling most of the shots. They like being led and courted. It makes the relationship feel lighter, easier, and more collaborative.

Obviously, we need to strike a balance between the guy that calls all the shots and the one that doesn't call any of the shots. We need to be cautious to not take these to either extreme and to find a middle ground that works best for the relationship.

Date nights are an easy lay up to take the lead. If you are going to start this process of leading more and making more decisions, start with the "Be ready by 6:00 p.m. on Friday for a date night. I have reservations for something fun and active, so wear workout clothes. After that, I have a place picked out where we can grab dinner, but don't worry—what you are wearing to the activity will be just fine. The kids are staying at my parents' for the night. Can't wait to pick you up!"

We have been doing this with men in The Dad Edge Alliance Mastermind for years, especially if it's been a while since the couple has had a date night. We have easily seen men do this hundreds of times, and I have yet to see a negative outcome. In fact, it's always met with excitement and anticipation on her end. This is because when we have a date night planned, it does three distinct things.

First, there is the anticipation and excitement of the upcoming date night for both you and her. Think of the last time you had something exciting evening planned on your calendar for both of you. You looked forward to it all week. Knowing that there was some fun and connection coming at the end of the week made the week feel easier to handle. When we know we have something fun on the horizon, it makes everything (even the challenges) feel a bit easier.

Second, there is the enjoyment of the event itself. Once we get to our date destination (dinner, activity, gathering, or really anything fun), we can simply kick back and just enjoy it. We can immerse ourselves (and each other) into the moment and enjoy the connection. It can feel euphoric to connect and communicate like we did in the beginning of our relationship.

Third, there are the amazing memories and connections that we make on the date itself that we can enjoy for days or even weeks after the date. Some of the best memories Jessica and I have ever made were on date nights.

When it comes to other decisions in the marriage or family, if we aren't going to lead, it's still important to collaborate or give an opinion. For years, Jessica has been the one to decorate our entire house. She has made nearly every decision from paint colors, to flooring, themes of rooms, accent items, and things we hang on the walls. She does an amazing job at it. To be honest, she is insanely skilled at decorating. She can take a blank room with nothing but white walls and make it look like something on HGTV. She can take a disastrous teenage boy room and turn it into a masculine sanctuary where my boys love it so much, they never want to leave.

I was not born with her gift. I have no interior décor sense at all. In fact, if you give me a blank room, I wouldn't know where to start. Same thing if you gave me a room that needed a complete overhaul. However, one thing has been constant—she wants and needs my input. She desires my opinion. By giving your opinion and point of view, you are still leading. Most women do not want a "whatever you want" type of man. They truly want our input and point of view.

13 NEVER BE AFRAID TO ASK FOR WHAT YOU WANT, NEED, OR DESIRE

> *"If you don't go after what you want, you will never have it. If you don't ask, the answer is always no. If you don't step forward, you're always in the same place."*
>
> — Nora Roberts

Over the past several years, I have worked with thousands of men. I have had the honor and privilege of hearing the origin stories of men's lives. I have heard about struggles and overcoming adversity. I have heard countless stories of men's childhoods—from the good to the traumatic. I have heard how men win in their marriages through communication, connection, and intimacy. I have also heard how men struggle with winning in their marriages. I've heard about parenting wins and unforgettable moments with men and their kids. I've also heard horror stories of how men have lost their patience and did something they regret in rage. To date,

I can honestly say I have heard just about all of it. I no longer get surprised with anything I hear that men experience.

There is one thing that scares men (even men who have been married for 10, 15, or 20-plus years). The fear of rejection is at the top of the list. Most of us remain quiet when it comes to the things we need, want, or desire in the relationship. When we think of needs, wants, and desires, many of us automatically think about things in the bedroom. Desires we want in the bedroom are certainly included, but not the be-all and end-all. There are a variety of other needs, wants, and desires that men never share out loud related to parenting, finances, goals for the future, our faith, time with friends, and even time with family. Most of us keep these needs, wants, and desires close to our chests for a variety of reasons.

First, we view our needs as selfish. We don't want to burden others (especially our wives) with what we want because men inherently want to serve. We want to be the ones to provide, not the ones that are takers. There is a level of guilt that is associated with asking for what we want because most of us have been trained since childhood to be the ones that give. Don't get me wrong; it's our job and duty to be providers, leaders, and protectors, but it can also be dangerous if we aren't communicating some of the things we need most in relationships. When we constantly serve, we sometimes pour from an empty cup as a result.

Second, we don't want to come across as "needy." I have yet to meet a man who is content with being a needy man. In fact, most of us consciously try to avoid being needy at all costs. We don't want to be the one that is taking in the relationship because we constantly want to serve and give.

The third and most common reason we don't ask for what we want is because of fear of rejection. The fear of rejection is a deep wound for most men, whether we admit it or not. When we are rejected, it brings up feelings of unworthiness, feelings of potential abandonment, and feelings of not being enough in the relationship. It brings up our deepest, darkest fears of isolation; that the ones we love most will leave us. These feelings run the deep in all human beings, not just men. A man's three basic needs are to feel respected, appreciated, and validated. When these needs aren't being met, we feel unfulfilled. When feelings of rejection emerge, these three basic needs feel threatened. As a result, we simply don't ask for what we want because we think that it's just not worth the risk.

Think of how often this has shown up in your life, even before marriage. Many of us avoided asking out that girl liked for so long because we didn't want to be rejected. Some of us avoided applying for colleges because we didn't want to risk getting the rejection letter in the mail. Many of us didn't try out for a sport we wanted to play because we didn't want to risk getting cut from the team. Perhaps you can relate to the feelings associated with getting picked last for a team when you were in gym class in school. The feelings of rejection run long and deep in our lives, and we avoid the pain at all costs.

The psychology behind this whole thing is that we are tied to the outcome, or the end result. We didn't ask that girl out in the past because we were tied to the outcome of her answer. If it was a "yes," we were good enough and worthy. If it was a "no," we weren't good enough, and then we would start to question if we were good enough in all other areas of our lives. We didn't apply to the college we wanted because we were tied to the end result of the approval or rejection letter. If we got in, we were smart enough. If we got rejected, we weren't smart enough. If tried out for sports team and you made it, you were strong or athletic enough. If you got cut, you weren't and began questioning other areas of your life. Same goes for marriage. If you ask your wife for what you want in the bedroom and she obliges, you are accepted, validated, good enough, and attractive enough. If she says no, it brings up all the feelings of rejection, unworthiness, and even the feeling of not being loved.

So, when it comes to asking what we want, what are we to do? Believe it or not, it's as simple as not tying the value of who we are and our worth to the outcome. It's not always about the outcome. What if instead of tying our worth and validation to the outcome, we tied our worth to the fact we made our request known? What if we actually got validation from the very act of asking for what we wanted instead of her answer? It's all about how we perceive situations like this. If we asked the girl out and simply got validation from the fact we had the courage to ask her instead of her answer, we could walk away from that situation knowing we tried and made our request known. If we tried out for the team and we got validation from the fact we tried versus whether or not we made it, we could walk away knowing we tried. If we applied for that college and we got validation from the fact we applied regardless of whether we made it in or not, we could walk away knowing we gave it all we had. The bottom line is this: it's living a life without regrets. It's doing the things we truly want and asking for the things we truly want without the feeling of regret that we never tried. Keep in mind, when it comes to life, we can only get hits if we are willing to step up to the plate and swing. The same goes for asking for what you need, want, and desire.

On final thought on this topic. When we can adopt this attitude of getting validation from making our requests known versus being tied to the outcomes, it makes our approach more confident and less needy. Our wives can sniff it out from a mile away if we feel uncertain. It comes across as unconfident and even unsafe. If you are confident and certain, she will feel that. So, be bold in asking for what you want in any aspect of your relationship. The answer might be yes, or it might be no. The bottom line is that you were bold and courageous enough to ask. Our wives (and people in general) admire boldness and confidence.

PART 3

FATHER

14 CONNECTION WITH KIDS

"You already have all you need to be a Great Dad!"

— Dr. Meg Meeker

We are starting with the quote above because it is SO IMPORTANT. This next section on fatherhood will be more in your face about a few things and for good reason. Read that quote from Dr. Meg above three more times before you read on. Let that quote really sink in.

One of the biggest problems with us dads is US! We are our own worst enemies. We constantly put ourselves down. We sabotage the hell out of our lives and our fatherhood journeys. For the most part, we are silently destroying our mental and emotional resilience. We constantly feel unworthy. We constantly criticize ourselves for mistakes that we make. We get frustrated with the way we execute fatherhood, and then we get frustrated that we are frustrated. It is an absolute vicious cycle of self-sabotage. We feel like we are doing a good job about 4 percent of the time, and the other 96 percent of the time we aren't living up to our expectations.

I have worked with thousands of men over the years, and this is the mentality. So if this rings true to you, you are not alone. You are the majority, not the minority. However, going through your fatherhood journey with this type of mentality (constantly self-criticizing, constantly self-sabotaging, constantly feeling unworthy) will destroy your enjoyment of being a father. Let's be real here; it will also destroy your marriage. Self-sabotage is a cancer that will infiltrate every aspect of your life if you don't learn the skills to end it.

So, before you read on, know this, own this, and live this...you already have everything you need to be a GREAT DAD. The missing piece is implementing critical skills that will set you apart from the majority of dads who destroy their relationships and enjoyment of fatherhood. So, let's get to the skills!

15 SKILL #1 - LOVE YOUR WIFE IN FRONT OF YOUR KIDS

> *"Husbands, love your wives well! Your children are noticing how you treat her. You are teaching your sons how they should treat women and you are teaching your daughters what they should expect from men."*
>
> — Dave Willis

I grew up with two very different examples and experiences growing up. My mom was married three times and dated several men in between her marriages. Every marriage (except the last one) was a complete disaster. I don't say that to blame my mother. I honestly believe my mom did the best she possibly could with the information she had and the journey she was on. Unfortunately, the outcomes were disastrous. I grew up seeing physical, mental, and emotional abuse. I also experienced hardcore emasculation of men in my mom's life. I saw men disrespected and emotionally abused. On the flip side, I saw men physically and emotionally abuse my mom. There was disrespect, radical anger, and drunken outbursts. My entire childhood felt extremely unsafe. There were times throughout my entire childhood that I dreaded being at home. I never knew when the next outburst was coming or the next physical altercation would erupt. I remember waking up to screaming, yelling, and fighting in the middle of the night. That was terrifying. A few times, when I was very young, I would cover my ears with my hands and scream into my pillow so I could drown out the fighting.

When there is an absence of love, affection, and safety, the kids truly suffer. They may or may not say it, but they know it's there and feel it. It affects them.

On the flip side, I got to see an amazing example of a man loving his wife growing up. As a young kid, my grandparents lived only one mile from us. I saw them all the time. Growing up, I saw them several times a week. For a stretch of fourth grade to eighth grade, I saw them every day. I would also spend the night on the weekends often. I loved it there. Looking back, there was good reason I loved it there. I got a front row-seat to an amazing example of a man and woman intentionally loving each other.

My grandma and grandpa were married 50 years before my grandpa passed away in 1998 at the age of 73 from heart complications. One thing I can tell you is they loved each other to the moon and back. I got to witness 23 years of their love before my grandpa passed away.

My grandpa was a blue-collar worker. He drove an 18-wheeler truck for 7 Up for over 40 years. I have never seen anyone work so hard in my life. He started his day at 3:00 a.m. every single day to get to the station and get on the road. He did that so he could make it home for dinner every night. He could have easily slept until 5:00 a.m. or 6:00 a.m., but he wouldn't have made it home until 7:00 p.m. or 8:00 p.m. If that was the case, he would have missed dinner with his family every night, and that just wasn't acceptable for him. On the weekends you would find him doing some gardening in the summer heat or cutting his grass. He was always moving and making things around him better.

The true gift I got to witness growing up was watching this man love his wife, and he did it VERY WELL. Not only did he love my grandma very well, but he did it publicly. He constantly hugged her and kissed her. He always told her how beautiful she was. I literally heard it and saw it every day. On weekends, my grandma and grandpa always had morning coffee together. They sat next to each other. My grandpa would randomly grab her hand, look right in her eyes, smile, and say, "I love you."

My grandma would light up, squeeze his hand back, and say, "I love you too." Most importantly, those weren't just words. If you were in the room, you felt their love. There was never a doubt in anyone's mind how much they loved each other. There was never a doubt how much my grandpa loved her. He constantly told her. He constantly complimented her. He made sure she knew it. Most importantly, he made sure he loved her in front of his family.

Being in that environment was so different than my home. My grandparents' home was a safe haven for me growing up. I knew there was safety there. I knew their relationship was solid. I knew she came first in his life. She came before his kids and grandkids. Nothing came between them. Because of that, he made everyone in the family feel loved, supported, and safe.

Many of us think that we must put our kids before our wives. That makes sense to us because our kids are more dependent on us than our wives. However, I encourage you to put your wife before your kids. You and her are the foundation of your family. If the foundation isn't solid, the house will not be secure.

Loving our wives intentionally and in front of the kids will do several positive things for the entire family.

1. When we love our wives publicly (compliment her, be affectionate with her, treat her with respect, listen to her), in front of our kids, it makes our kids feel safe and loved as well.

2. This teaches our daughters how a man should love them. Keep in mind, YOU are the first man in your daughter's life. She will hold every man she dates or marries to the standard you set.

3. This teaches our sons how to love a woman. When a young man grows up seeing how to love a woman, you are giving him a front row-seat to the most critical relationship skills.

4. When the husband and wife have a secure, loving relationship, it will elevate the love of the entire family.

When we become fathers (and mothers), it's easy to put our marriages on the backburner to take care of the kids first. There will be stages (especially when they are very young) of our kids' lives where this makes sense, but overall, keep your marriage front and center. You both are the foundation of the house that the family is built on.

16 SKILL #2 - PATIENCE IS A SKILL, NOT A FEELING... SO LEARN THE SKILL

> *"A moment of patience in a moment of anger saves you a hundred moments of regret."*
> — Author Unknown

Ask any of us what we struggle with most, and we will tell you, if we are being honest, it's patience. Being a dad will test all of us and humble the best of us. When our kids act out, we have a tough time being patient. If we have been a dad for any amount of time, we have had situations we wish could take back. We have words that we have said that we wish we could take back. We can't go back and change the past, but we can learn and implement skills that we will prevent these things in the future.

The origin of The Dad Edge came out of absolute darkness. It didn't start with a beautiful epiphany where I suddenly learned all the skills to be a more patient father. The Dad Edge started with a dark moment with my second-born son who was only four years old at the time. It's a story I am not proud of.

As you know by now, my childhood wasn't sunshine and rainbows. There was a lot of abuse and darkness. I was emotionally and physically abused by father figures that would be in and out of my life. When I became a father for the first time in 2006, I swore that a repeat of my childhood wouldn't happen on my watch. I'm happy to say that up until 2012, there wasn't a serious dark incident. However, what I can tell you is that things were far from amazing.

Back then, I wasn't nearly the man I am today. I wasn't very patient with my boys. I was quick to raise my voice. I didn't hit them. I didn't call them names. But I also didn't show up the way I do now. I was "half in/half out" when it came to being present and raising them. I didn't know what I was doing and felt pretty lost. I was heavily involved in my career. At the time, I was in medical device sales. I made a great living. I was great at my job. I won sales awards almost every year during that career. I was promoted over and over. I was exceling in my career yet barely meeting expectations at home. I wanted so badly to show up big for my boys but just had no clue how to do it. Looking back on why I was so successful with my career, it was because I was always eager to learn and grow! I constantly read books on sales, leadership, working with customers, etc. I went to conferences and constantly educated myself through online training. I was doing the opposite in my parenting and marriage. I didn't read books. I didn't learn new skills. I had a perception that if I needed extra help in those departments, I was broken or something was wrong with me. After all, shouldn't parenting and marriage come naturally?

The answer is "NO!" The love for our family comes naturally. The motivation to protect and provide comes naturally. However, the skills are what I lacked. Looking back, I literally shake my head and wonder why I would think such a foolish thing.

I can honestly tell you it was my ego that got in the way. My ego kept telling me I shouldn't need extra help or I should not have to learn and grow to be a solid father and husband. HUGE MISS! As a result, I simply disengaged from my boys for the first six years of their lives. I was there physically, but I wasn't there emotionally.

Getting back to that dark moment on an evening back in 2012... It had been one of those days where work was long, and it wasn't a good day. I was frustrated because I had lost a big customer to a competitor. The result of losing this customer was a huge hit to my income and to my confidence. On top of it, Jessica and I had an argument earlier in the day (which was the norm). At this point in our marriage, we didn't get along like we do now. At the time, I was making good money, but we still weren't doing the best in our finances because quite frankly, we didn't know what we were doing. On top of everything else, we were getting ready to put our house on the market to sell. However, we didn't know exactly where we were going to move. I went downstairs and decided to work on packing. I started with the boys' playroom. There were toys scattered everywhere. The entire room looked like a toy explosion. There are a few things that frustrate me. One is massive messes and total disorganization (which basically described our boy's playroom). Another one is the stress of moving. I was in a headspace of absolute anger. Anger because I lost a huge customer that would now impact our livelihood. Anger because I now had to figure out how to explain this situation to my boss and upper-management team. I would also have to explain this to Jessica. This was just the cherry on top of the sundae. At the time, we were just existing. We weren't very close. Our intimacy was few and far between. We didn't have a deep connection or communication. On top of it, we were getting ready to move, and the house was a disorganized mess. In that moment, I felt tremendous frustration. As I started packing up the boys' toys, trying to find pieces of one set of toys to match with another, I found myself just getting more and more frustrated. My life wasn't bad, but it wasn't nearly as good as I thought it would be. I worked for about three hours packing up everything in the boys' playroom. I was tired. I was angry. I was frustrated. At this point, Mason came downstairs to play in his playroom, where he found all of his toys had been packed up. I knew he wanted to play with some of his toys, so I went ahead and unpacked a few random toys to keep him busy. In a defeated tone, I told him to play with the toys I had gotten out and to not unpack anything I had just spent the entire evening packing up. I told him I was going to take a break and come back in about 30 minutes.

I went upstairs, where I simply sat on the couch and sat in silence. My head was spinning because I started thinking about how I was going to tell Jessica that our next few financial months would be a struggle and we would have to be really careful with money. As a men and as providers, we dread these conversations. I didn't have the talk with her that night; instead, I just sat in silence and allowed even more thoughts of scarcity to control my mind. I started wondering if this was the start of me losing more customers and losing more income. *Maybe my boss will put me on a performance-improvement plan.... I might be pushed out of my job and let go....* I started wondering how we would buy our next house. I could only imagine the stress and pressure this would put on our already fragile marriage that was hanging on by a thread. Thoughts that go unchecked and unmanaged can truly run amok in our minds and hearts if allowed to do so.

After about 30 minutes, I decided to go downstairs and tell Mason it was time for bed. As I walked downstairs, I felt overwhelmed by the frustrations of the day. When I turned the corner and entered the boys' playroom, I saw that he had opened up several of the boxes, and toys that I had spent hours packing were scattered all over the floor. Immediately, I felt so much anger. In that moment, my darkest hour as a father was upon me. I started yelling at him and told him that he was not to pull any other toys out of boxes besides what I took out for him. I grabbed him by his arm and spanked him. What happened next was the part I am not proud of. I had spanked him so hard that he lost his balance and fell to the ground. Immediately, I was stunned at what I just did. I couldn't believe that I reacted with so much anger. I had promised myself that I wouldn't hit my kids. I had promised that I wouldn't do the things to them that were done to me. I immediately knew what I just did was wrong. I went to help him up, and when I extended my arms to pick him up, he looked at me like I was a monster. There was a look of fear in his eyes that I had never seen. That look shot right though my heart and literally broke it. In that moment, I not only saw my son who was scared of me, but I also saw me at his age. I was beaten a lot growing up. I was always terrified of being hit and I lived in fear for years. I saw that same look in his eyes.

As he cried, I picked him up. I held him. He was crying and shaking. I was beyond devastated. *What did I just do?* I eventually calmed him down. I apologized. I took him upstairs and got him ready for bed. I tucked him in and apologized again. Looking up at me, he said: "It's OK, Daddy." Kids are resilient. More resilient than most of us.

I went back downstairs to my office. As I walked down the stairs, I could feel the massive guilt and shame on my heart and shoulders. It felt like 100 pounds on my back. The basement was dark. I entered my office, and the lights were off. I sat at my desk in the dark and just started to cry. I hated myself for what I did. I couldn't get the look on his face out of my mind. *How could I* do that? How could I hurt my son who I was supposed to protect? What's wrong with me? Why did this happen? Why couldn't I find the patience or grace? After all, it really wasn't that big of a deal in the grand scheme of things.

As I sat in my office in the dark, I didn't want to think about it anymore. So, I did what most adults do when we want to escape. I turned on my computer and got on Facebook. When things go bad in our lives, one of the things we turn to is a way to distract and escape.

The Surrender

With tears in my eyes and scrolling through everyone else's highlight reel, I noticed a button in the lefthand corner of the Facebook home page. It said: "Create A Page." I have no idea what came over me, but I honestly believe it was divine intervention. I had no idea nor any intention of what the future was going to hold, but in that moment, hitting that button not only changed my life, my family, and my marriage, but it also became a movement that would go worldwide. I hit that button, and the screen reloaded for me to name the page. Without even a moment to ponder, the four words "THE GOOD DAD PROJECT" rolled off my mind and heart on and onto that keyboard.

Creating that page was a surrender. I didn't create the page for a following. I created that page because I wanted to learn how to be a better father, husband, and man. As I sat there and looked at the page, I considered the option of learning something new every single day. In that moment, it hit me that with anything that I was ever good at in life, I had to learn skills, implement them, and practice them daily. I was great at my job, but it was only because I was constantly learning. I was pretty fit, but only because I constantly worked at it and learned ways to be healthier. I was good at martial arts, but only because I went to class and was coached by my instructor. As I reflected on anything I ever exceled in, I realized there was always an investment on my part of time and/or resources. As I thought about my marriage, I realized I had put more time, effort, and money into our wedding day than I did our marriage. I realized as a father, I had put more time and effort into making my children than I did learning how to raise them.

The surrender was a moment of admitting I had no idea what to do and how to navigate being a father and husband. It actually felt amazing. For once I didn't feel the burden of thinking I had to know everything about being a good dad and husband. I knew in that moment, I could simply start learning and growing. Why would parenting or marriage be any different than any other skill I learned and excelled in?

Breaking Down Patience

If there is anything I have learned over the past 10 years of leading this mission, coaching thousands of men, and being a student myself is that patience isn't something that comes natural to human beings. Human beings by nature are not patient beings. We seek quick fixes, comfort, and immediate gratification.

Having more patience for our kids, our families, our work demands, and even ourselves is extremely difficult. We expect that patience should come naturally because we are parents. It's actually the opposite. If we really think about our lives overall, there is never a time when our lives get more complex and demanding than when we get married, have kids, work full time, and try to take on every other demand that comes our way. Yet we expect our patience and resilience will adapt accordingly. Not the case.

To really hone this skill, we have to understand that patience is a skill and practice it. We also have to realize that if we going to implement the practice, we have to trust the process and not always be tied to the fact that we will do it flawlessly at all times. There will be times that we lose our patience, even if we learn new skills to optimize it.

So, let's break it down.

What Is Patience?

Patience is defined as the capacity to accept or tolerate delay, trouble, or suffering without getting angry or upset.

Ask any parent—patience is the number one thing that we all struggle with most. As parents, we are constantly tested with work, parenting, coaching, maintaining a home, emotional/physical care of our kids, creating a thriving marriage, mastering our finances, climbing the corporate ladder/leading a business, and maintaining our own self-care and health. We have so many demands on our time, and it feels like people need something from us every minute of every day.

The shortage of patience can show up in several ways:

- Physically – we can literally feel a shortage of patience in our physical bodies. This can be seen when we feel agitated, we breathe shallow, and we tense our muscles in our neck and shoulders. We can even have headaches and issues with digestion.

- Mentally/Emotionally – a shortage of patience can wreak havoc on our mental and emotional health. When our mind is in constant fight/flight mode, it can wear us down and make us incapable of emotionally/mentally handling things that come our way.

- External Relationships – we can take our stress out on others. We can even isolate ourselves from loved ones because we feel shame, guilt, or frustration that we aren't showing up the way we know we can.

- Internal (relationship with ourselves) – when we don't have patience (even for ourselves), we can speak poorly to ourselves (even when no one else can hear). It's a vicious cycle of losing our patience with someone else externally and then losing patience with ourselves internally with shame and guilt.

Think about the following reflection questions:

1. Reflect on some of the most difficult situations you encounter as a dad and husband. Think of situations that push your abilities to respond positively or with calm to the environment around you. Why is creating more patience important for you as a father/husband?

2. In what areas of your life would you like to become more patient?

3. What would this allow you to do more of?

Patience Starts in the Morning

Many of us don't realize that our morning routine can set the stage for an epic day or it can be the beginning of disaster. I fully know that many of us are sick and tired of hearing about morning routines. So many people post on social media about their morning gratitude, mindfulness, workouts, journaling, planning for the day, their goals, priorities, spiritual reflections, and so on. Many of us are fatigued with the amount of variety and options for morning routines. I get it. I was there once as well.

However, over the past several years, I've seen incredible benefits with my morning routine and the routines of hundreds of other men. I have more clarity. I am more productive. I am able to manage my day versus my day managing me. Over the past seven years and 800 podcast experts, I can say with all confidence that some of the most successful and happy people on the planet stick to some sort of morning routine and they keep it sacred. Nothing deters them or gets in the way of their morning routine.

Here's what I can tell you; whether you have a morning routine or not, you are most likely doing the things I used to do first thing in the morning, which are the very things that set our day up for negative outcomes. For example, if I can encourage you to do one thing, even if you don't have a morning routine, it is NOT to engage in any type of media whatsoever for at least the first 90 minutes of waking up. That means no news, no phone, no email, no social media, no YouTube, etc. You're likely using your phone as an alarm clock. When you go to pick up your phone, turn the alarm off, and get out of bed, your home screen already has your attention. Maybe you see how many emails are in your inbox. Perhaps you see the number of text messages that came in from the night before. You could also be seeing how many notifications you have on social media. It could also be that CNN, the *Washington Post*, or the *Huffington Post* just launched that new news article that the world as we know it is coming to an end or there is economic unrest. It truly doesn't matter what type of notification we see; we are now triggered, and we haven't even made it to the bathroom or wiped the sleep from our eyes.

When we wake up first thing in the morning, our brain is still in a beta state. We are vulnerable to being triggered into fight or flight. That's not to say we are going to run or fight someone, but it does mean that we are triggered by what we see. Sometimes it doesn't even have to be something negative. It can be something as simple as the volume of notifications that come in between news, texts, emails, social, calendar meeting requests, etc. We have an immediate feeling of overwhelm.

Think about this for a moment. Twenty years ago, we never had access to the volume of information we have at our fingertips now. Twenty years ago, we were never this accessible to everyone on the planet. If we have a phone, anyone can reach us at any minute of every single day. This can be extremely overwhelming and can wreak havoc on how we show up and how much patience we have for others, for problems, and even ourselves.

If you truly want to wreck your emotional resilience for the day, then keep checking your phone first thing in the morning. If you want to start the day off with stress and overwhelm, then keep checking your phone first thing in the morning.

If you want to change the way you go through your day, and if you don't have a morning routine and don't want to implement one, at the very least, take a breather from any type of media for at least 60 minutes (90 minutes is ideal) every morning upon waking up.

On the flip side, if you are serious about wanting to start a morning routine, I will share mine here and all the benefits. You might not like the time I wake up every day, but it works for me, and the benefits outweigh the cons.

4:05 a.m. – Wake (no snooze on the alarm). I thank God for waking me up and giving me another day (puts me right into gratitude and spirituality). No phone and no media.

4:15 a.m. – Get dressed, take my supplements and vitamins, and slam 25 ounces of cold water. Our bodies haven't had hydration for about 6 – 8 hours, so water is a MUST!

4:30 a.m. – Pick up my workout partner. Being honest here, I'm tired in the morning. Having an accountability partner and knowing my workout partner is waiting on me gets me out the door.

4:45 a.m. – I'm on the treadmill, running for 20 – 25 minutes to get the blood flowing and body moving.

5:15 a.m. – Weight training. I work out Monday through Saturday, every single morning. Resistance training has many physical benefits, but the mental and emotional benefits are where it's at for me.

6:15 a.m. – 15-minute sauna. I jump in the sauna after a workout to sweat out toxins. There is a laundry list of benefits of sauna.

6:40 a.m. – On my way back home to take my two older boys to school.

6:55 a.m. – Take my two older boys to school. We talk about our day ahead and gratitude. This gets all of us in a state of gratitude and connection.

7:15 a.m. – Back home. Brew coffee. Begin 10 minutes of Wim Hof breathwork. The benefits of Wim Hof breathwork are absolutely life changing. I feel insanely clear, de-stressed, fully oxygenized, and ready for my day. I also do 10 minutes of silent meditation or prayer.

7:40 a.m. – Greet my two younger boys and talk to them about their day and what has them most excited.

8:00 a.m. – Younger boys leave for school, and I jump in the shower.

8:20 a.m. – In my office with my planner. I write out three things I am grateful for, my three priorities of the day, and my critical tasks (the needle movers). I plan the entire day. I know what times I will be meeting with clients, recording a podcast, checking emails, updating social media, and plans for the evening. When I plan like this, I am planning to manage my day, not for my day to manage me.

8:45 a.m. – Now I can check my phone or device.

Now, I fully understand this morning routine is in-depth and it's over the course of nearly five hours, but you can see how much is accomplished before 9:00 a.m. and how I incorporate the most important things for my day and my family into this routine. What I can tell you about this morning routine is it sets me up for success. I can be fully present in every moment because I have a plan for the day. I operate in containers of intentional time. I know that you have a ton of things that are constantly fighting for your attention. You have work, emails, texts, work projects, deadlines, social media, kids' activities, social life, obligations, your own self-care, your family obligations and quality time, etc. We all have that. Many of us are managed by our day instead of us managing our day. We feel consumed by the distractions and end our days feeling exhausted and even overwhelmed. The end result? This type of busyness will erode our patience. It will literally devastate it. Many of us wonder why we have knee-jerk reactions to problems in our lives or when our kids are testing us. A lot of it has to do with the way our days run us into the ground. If we start the day with a solid morning routine, it becomes a launching pad for our lives and sets us up for more emotional resilience.

So, if you want more patience in your life, a solid morning routine is a very effective (if not the most effective) start.

Creating Space Between Trigger and Response

Controlling our actions and emotions is the ability to manage the way we respond to what is happening. The only actions (and reactions) we can control are our own. In other words, the world can be in chaos around us, and we can still have the ability to respond with calm if we so choose. Being really honest here, we can choose calm if we are trained to do so.

Before we jump into the tactics of better responses in the heat of moments where absolute chaos is unfolding, it's important to understand a few comparisons to how we respond to other things in our life that are different than how we respond with our kids.

We have all been in situations with our kids where they have either done something wrong or they are having a meltdown. We see them do something and we are triggered to anger quickly. As a result, we then react without thinking. We say something we regret or even do something we regret like I did with my own son.

This examples below serve as a good gut check for how we can look at situations with our kids a bit differently. Would you speak to your people in your place of work the same as your kids in the heat of a chaotic situation? For a minute, think of your place of work. Think of your boss, coworkers, or even customers. We have all been in situations in the workplace where we are triggered and have the temptation to react. Maybe your boss said something to you that made you angry? Perhaps you had a coworker that threw you under the bus? Maybe it was a customer that was being difficult? The situation really doesn't matter, because chances are you didn't yell, scream, or say something you regretted. You were able to create space between the situation and your response. You most likely responded to the situation with a level of calm and professionalism despite how much you wanted to fly off the handle.

I had a fantastic guest, Drew Tupper (author of *Peaceful Parenting*), use this exact comparison on the show. He simply asked, "Would you talk to people you work with the same way you would talk to your kids when things get heated?" The question was so simple, and it stopped me in my tracks. The answer was, of course, "NO!" So, why do we fly off the handle at our kids compared to other areas of our life where we have demonstrated restraint? One of the reasons is the consequences of losing our tempers can result in the loss of our livelihood. Similar things can be said for consequences with our kids, however. Yelling at our kids might not take away our livelihood, but it will definitely take away other important factors in our life. We will vastly decrease the level of psychological safety our kids feel with us. In other words, our kids might view us as an unstable foundation. They will think twice about opening up to us as they get older. They will want to spend less time with us and more time with others. They will feel pushed away and unworthy. There are devasting effects of us constantly losing our cool with our kids. Being calm in our responses is the absence of solid discipline. We can actually have both calm and discipline. We can respond with calm when situations get heated with our kids yet have solid lines of discipline, structure, boundaries, and consequences.

Below is a list of ways we can create space between stimulus and response:

- Breathe. This sounds very simple, but it is foundational. When we are stressed, we "chest breathe," and that will actually agitate the sympathetic nervous system (fight or flight). Taking a moment to take three to five deep breaths will actually activate our parasympathetic nervous system (rest and digest). When we activate this system, we physically and mentally calm ourselves. It sounds simple, but most effective measures are simple!

- Ask yourself why this situation is making you so angry. Emotions like anger are neither bad nor good...they just are. Understanding why you are angry will give you clarity around what is actually showing up for you. When we have more clarity, we have more calm.

- Detach from outcomes. When we are in a highly stressful state of anger or stress, it's usually because we feel a loss of control and things are not happening the way we wanted.

- Prepare for obstacles. One of my favorite quotes, by Louis Pasteur, is: "Chance favors the prepared mind." Life will not always go as expected. When we are prepared for different scenarios (even the worst-case scenarios), we can prepare for a response ahead of time instead of being taken by surprise. A perfect example of this is me being prepared for a dinner with my four boys and wife (story below).

- Give yourself grace when you lose your cool. One of the worst things we can do is add insult to injury when we do mess up and react in a way that isn't ideal. When we do mess up, we can give ourselves grace and start anew. Remember, creating patience starts with how we speak to ourselves when no one else is listening.

What to Do When We Are Triggered in the Moment
Think about the last time you lost your patience and reacted in anger or even outrage. The body and mind were most likely giving

you warning signs before the outburst or reaction even happened. I like to call these warning signs. For the most part, if we are really tuned into our mentality and emotions, we can feel ourselves getting triggered. We can even start to feel the warning signs that an outburst is coming. It can feel like a volcano before it erupts. Tremendous pressure builds from the inside before the eruption. Think of the last time you vomited. You felt the warning signs and the pressure building. You knew it was coming. We know full well when an eruption of emotions is coming. We know full well when a projectile vomit of emotions is coming.

Here are some warning signs that could be happening before we lose our cool:

1. Sweaty palms
2. Incomplete thoughts/defeating self-talk
3. Shallow breathing (chest breathing)
4. Racing heart
5. Clenched fists
6. Grinding teeth
7. Pacing
8. Tightness in chest and shoulders

There are several more that can give you warning signs, but the above are the most common.

The most important thing to realize is it's OK to have these emotions. It's human to have these emotions and warning signs. Where the rubber meets the road is knowing what to do in the moment to avoid a terrible outcome that we regret. When the warning signs come, there are things we can do to CREATE SPACE between a reaction we regret and a response that is more in line with the results we want.

When we feel any of the above warning signs happening, there are a few things we can do to interrupt a knee-jerk negative reaction and respond more positively. It sounds simple, but all we really need to do is create a window of four to six seconds before we respond. A slight distraction, if you will.

- Count backwards from 50 in increments of three. It sounds too simple to actually work, but the simplicity is what makes it effective. "50,47,44,41,38, etc." If these feel uncomfortable, and it takes a bit of thinking, THAT'S A GOOD SIGN! That means it's working.

- Diaphragm breathing instead of chest breathing. Deep breathing with our gut instead of our chest will activate the parasympathetic nervous system (rest and digest). We can physically calm our body and mind down just with our breath. Don't believe me? Try it.

- Snap your fingers with your left hand while wiggling your right pinky toe. It sounds absolutely crazy, but you need to concentrate and focus in order to pull this off. It seems simple. Try it! Not so simple. Again, what we are doing here is buying time and space of about four to six seconds to calm down instead of reacting.

- Count 10 things in the room and name them quietly in your mind. When my kids are doing something that isn't harmful, yet it is just annoying me, I still have a tendency to want to yell at times. When I can simply look around the room, identify 10 objects, name them quietly to myself, it buys me the time I need to ensure I don't react in a way I would otherwise regret.

There are several other things that we can do in the moment of being triggered; however, the above four are the easiest and most effective. I have no doubt you might be thinking that these may never work or they are just too simple. Again, their simplicity is what makes them elegant and effective.

Don't SHOULD On Yourself

Guilt, judgement, and shame don't serve us an any way if we simply use these feelings to beat ourselves up. Typically, these emotions will result in self-sabotage and us giving up. Many of us are good at "shoulding" on ourselves. In fact, most of us are great at taking huge steaming piles of SHOULD all over ourselves—meaning even when we have normal human emotions like anger, sadness, overwhelm, and feelings of just being stressed out, we immediately say things to ourselves like:

"I SHOULDN'T be angry! I SHOULD be happier! I must be weak!"

"I need to man up! I SHOULDN'T be sad right now!"

"I SHOULDN'T be overwhelmed or stressed! I SHOULD be able to take on anything!"

Gents, let me say this here and now. These statements are LIES! They are absolute LIES that lead to SELF-SABOTAGE. When we speak this way to ourselves, we are pouring salt in an open wound.

Remember, we are all human. You are allowed to feel emotions such as anger, sadness, and overwhelm. It doesn't make you less of man, husband, or human being. It makes you HUMAN. Remember, emotions are neither bad nor good...they just are.

The solution is ensuring you are implementing the right strategies and tactics when situations arise and when you are being tested.

Bottom line: don't SHOULD on yourself. Implement the tactics of creating more patience and trust the process. When you mess up, review the process and understand what you missed so you can learn for the next situation. No one ever got great at anything by self-sabotage, so stop doin' that SHIT!

Get Realistic!

Being completely realistic here, mistakes and blowups will still happen. Simply because we learn a new strategy and tactic doesn't mean we will be completely bulletproof and mistakes will never be made again. Learning new tactics and strategies simply means we can make fewer mistakes and pivot to solutions faster. Many of us are under the impression that if we learn something new and evolve, it somehow makes us immune to negative moments moving forward. That's not the case. It means our success rate for positive outcomes will improve and we can learn how to get out of a bad moment faster and more efficiently.

Think of it another way. For a moment, think of your favorite professional athlete. Some of us admire a certain baseball player. Does that baseball player bat one thousand every time they are up to bat? Think of your favorite UFC fighter. Will he (or she) go undefeated for their entire career? What about your favorite quarterback? Does he complete every single pass thrown? Absolutely not to all of the above! We are no different. So why do we hold ourselves to a perfect standard and then beat ourselves up when mistakes are made. It's not a realistic point of view when we really think about it.

So, what do the most successful people do? They simply review what is working and what isn't. They also trust the process and they remain disciplined to their practice. So, know this moving forward, it doesn't help you to self-sabotage yourself. It doesn't help you to wallow in guilt, shame, or blame. The only thing that will help is learning what was missed and making pivots to your practice.

I've been coaching men for years and I can tell you that mistakes do happen constantly when we are trying to grow and evolve. The most effective tool when learning anything new is using after-action reviews. Most of the time, when mistakes are made, we can learn what was missed or what needs to be tweaked when we look at the situation. Most of the time, when we lose our patience and we have a blow up, we missed or overlooked something in the process.

Upon review of a situation, usually we find that we missed our morning routine and dove straight into our devices. Perhaps we saw a headline that sparked some serious stress or we got an email from our boss that a fire needed to be put out. Other times, we overlooked our self-care in some way. Sometimes, it can be that we simply had a knee-jerk reaction to a situation without creating any type of mental and emotional space before responding. In some cases, we have missed everything; our day started in a stressful state, and we never did anything to interrupt the pattern. Nevertheless, it's important to identify what was missed, what lessons we learned, and how we will be better in the future. For the most part, the only thing that gets in the way of our learning and being better is our own guilt, shame, and blame. Guilt, shame, and blame don't serve any of us.

17 SKILL 3 – KIDS SPELL "L-O-V-E," "T-I-M-E"

"Children spell love with four letters: T-I-M-E..."
— Max Lucado

If we truly want a connection with our kids, we have to understand how they receive love and what they need from us. Many of are spending a ton of our valuable time chasing our careers so we can provide for our kids. Many of us view our value and our worth by what we provide. Providing for our families is wired in our genetic makeup. We take pride in doing it! Ask almost any man, and he will tell you that one of his greatest fears is not being able to provide for his family.

At times we can confuse what providing is all about. Yes, we need to provide basic needs (food, shelter, and clothing), but most importantly, we have to provide TIME. Our kids don't care what kind of car we drive. They don't care how much money is in our bank account or retirement. For the most part, they don't really care what stuff they have or brand of clothes they wear. Sure, some of them will tell us they want the latest and greatest gadget, shoes, or device. However, at the end of the day, what they truly value is the time and connection.

The simple things are usually the most effective. Men, in general, are extreme beings. We want to go all in and do something big. If it isn't big enough to meet our standards, we usually don't do it. This can hinder the connection with our kids, because our kids simply want our time doing simple things. Playing catch, playing dress up (if you have daughters), hiking, fishing, going to watch a sporting event, and even learning something new can be incredible bonding experiences.

If you have multiple kids, one of the greatest gifts we can give them is the gift of one-on-one time. If they have to constantly share their time with you with a sibling, then one-on-one time is GOLD to them. If you don't believe me, just ask them; they will tell you the same. We don't get as many opportunities as we think. Most of us are under the impression that we have 18 years with our kids, so we believe we have plenty of time. We actually don't have that much time.

In September of 2019, I interviewed Todd Herman, bestselling author of *The Alter Ego Effect*. It was by far one of my favorite interviews to date on *The Dad Edge Podcast*. Todd is an author, performance advisor, and entrepreneur. For 22 years, his training company, Herman Performance Systems, has focused on helping achievers and ambitious people in sports and business achieve wildly outrageous goals while enjoying the process. His company has a suite of programs serving Olympic athletes, entrepreneurs, and leaders. He's been featured on the *Today Show*, *Sky Business News*, *CBC National News*, and in *Inc Magazine*.

The premise of his book is how human beings can unlock alter egos to achieve improved performance in athletics, work, relationships, parenting, mindset, and life.

When Todd came on the show, he shared a statistic that stopped me in my tracks. He stated that 80 percent of our one-on-one time with our kids is gone by the time they are 12. Reason being, friends and activities become more important from that age on. Think about it; when you were younger, at what age did you start pulling away from your family and want to spend more time with friends? It was right around that age. If I could give you any sense of urgency, it's to take full advantage of one-on-one time with your kids as soon as possible. It will elevate the connection for both of you. It will strengthen the bond for years to come. The more one-on-one time we invest with them at an early age, the more elevated the relationship will be over the years.

Personally, I am a BIG FAN of not only spending one-on-one time with my boys but also doing one-on-one trips with them. It isn't easy because I have four boys, but what I can tell you is I don't regret any of them. One-on-one trips get us out of the daily grind and away from everyday living. They get us out of our comfort zones with them and away from distractions. You will experience conversations and connections that you never thought possible. I started taking each one of my boys on a yearly one-on-one trip starting at the age of six years old. I am proud to say that I have a solid connection with each of my sons and when I look back on the launching pad of when things got really close and connected, it was always after that first one-on-one trip. It might feel like a tall order to schedule a one-on-one trip, but the ROI is well worth it for years to come.

18 SKILL #4 – CREATE AN ENVIRONMENT OF PSYCHOLOGICAL SAFETY SO YOUR KIDS WILL COME TO YOU WITH EVERYTHING

> *"Your honesty and ownership are celebrated and not shamed."*
>
> — Larry Hagner

When I was younger, I was terrified to tell my mom just about everything. Her reactions to situations were completely unpredictable. Sometimes she would take things well, but most of the time, she wouldn't. It didn't really matter what the situation was or what was happening; the reaction to anything negative was guilt, shame, blame, or pain. A lot of us who are my age were raised that way. We were terrified to tell our parents something for fear of the reaction and the ramifications. Maybe it was a poor grade on a test or perhaps some sort of wrongdoing, but no matter what it was, we wanted to keep things close to our chests for fear of reactions. For the most part, even our feelings were shamed or wrong if we didn't feel right about something or even questioned something. Our childhoods were what they were, and it's not bad nor good; it just was what it was. Our parents did the best they could with the information they had.

This generation of fathers is different. We have a deep desire not only to lead, provide, guide, and parent our kids, but we also want to have a deep, meaningful connection with them. We want our kids to come talk to us about everything that is going on in their lives. We want to not only share in the highlights of our kids' lives but also be there when shadows of the dark times emerge. It's easy for us to show up during the highlight reel of our kids' lives and share the big, meaningful things; it's a bit more complex and takes a bit more to show up for the dark times.

Most of us want our kids to come talk to us when they are facing darkness, mistakes they have made, or even dishonesty, but when our kids do something wrong, we have more of a tendency to react, punish, and shame.

Being real, I used to get so angry with my boys when their grades didn't meet expectations. I am not the parent who expects straight A's, but I do expect best effort to be put forward. In the past, I didn't expect anything less than B's. If C's were on the report card or progress report, it was usually followed by a huge lecture and a punishment until grades came up. When my boys would come home with poor grades on homework and tests, they would get a similar reaction with consequences. The lecture was usually filled with me shaming and guilting. It would look like "Why can't you take more time to study?" "Why aren't you putting forth your best effort?" "Why are you not getting this?" These really poor guilt-ridden questions were followed up by a punishment of some sort. The funny thing is the lectures and the punishments didn't work! I never really saw an improvement in grades or performance. In fact, they would either stay the same or go down even more. Not to mention, the connection with my kids became more compromised over time. I noticed they would come and talk to me less. They would hide their grades from me or they would go to their mom with bad news because she responded better than I did. So, not only did my actions not result in an improvement in school performance; they managed to distance the relationships I had with my kids and our connection.

Creating psychological safety isn't the absence of discipline. Instead, creating psychological safety is creating the environment where our kids feel safe but can also learn through natural consequences. They can also learn from how we guide them through conversation and questions. If we respond with calm voices to situations where we would otherwise get heated, we can create a more powerful learning environment.

The 3 Daily Questions That Will Create Psychological Safety

You're probably wondering: *How can I create this environment?* Creating an environment of psychological safety doesn't happen overnight. It happens with a daily practice that makes daily deposits every single day. The below practice is one of the simplest ways to create an elevated connection with your kids, and over time, you will notice they will come to you when they need advice or they need a safe place to land when things go wrong in their lives. I also map out the psychology behind each of these questions so you clearly understand the meaning and importance behind each of them.

QUESTION #1: "What was the best part of your day?"

Remember in the chapter titled "The Quality of Your Relationship Is Determined by the Quality of Your Questions" when I presented the most useless question of all: "How was your day?" I encourage you, in addition to not asking this to your wife, to not ask this question to your kids either.

We ask this question by habit and by default. We ask this question without even thinking about it. It's a really poor question that always gives us similar poor responses that create no connection whatsoever. We usually hear the same answers: "Good," "Fine," "Boring," "Crazy," etc. After that response, we usually just move on and wonder why we aren't connecting. Remember, the quality of our relationships depends on the quality of our questions.

When we tweak that question to "What was the best part of your day?", we are guiding our kids into gratitude, and now they not only have to answer the question, but they also have to tell a story. When we ask this question, we are triggering their brains to recall something that was a high-point moment of their day. They have to stop and think about a situation that was elevating for them. Maybe they set a new record running the 100-meter dash, or perhaps they got an A on their last test. It could be something about their friendships or relationships. At any rate, it doesn't matter because that question triggered an elevation in their energy and got them into a state of gratitude. Not to mention, they are now sharing that high-point moment with YOU! When we share joy, gratitude, and high-point moments with someone, it brings us closer together. This question also sends the message "I am interested in you!" to our kids. When we show that we are interested in the joyful moments our kids' experience, it brings the relationships and connections we have with them up several notches.

THE PURSUIT OF LEGENDARY FATHERHOOD

QUESTION #2: "What was the most challenging part of your day, and how did you get through it?" or "What did you fail at today, and what did you learn?"

This question right here is what psychological safety is all about! There are several psychological factors at play here, and it's a question that really sets the stage for the level of connection and safety our kids feel with us.

This question forces our kids to look at a low point of their day. They have to think about failures or challenges and how they faced them. Not only do they have to think about these situations, but now they are being invited to share them with you. When you ask this question, you have to be prepared for anything to come your way and respond with calm. There will be times you will ask this question and you will hear something that disappoints you greatly. Maybe they got caught doing something wrong at school or got a bad grade on a test. Perhaps it's something they aren't proud of, like they were picked last again to be on a team, and they don't want to share that shameful news with Dad. Deep down, our kids want Dad's approval and validation so badly. When they share a moment or a situation that they are ashamed of, they are really becoming very authentic and vulnerable. They are removing layers and showing us a side of them that they otherwise wouldn't.

In some situations, we (including me) have handled these things really poorly. I will never forget a time when one of my boys came home and told me he got a D on the science test.

Son: "Dad, I got a D on the science test today."

Me: "What do you mean you got a D on the test? I told you to study for that! Didn't I tell you that you needed to put in more time studying for that test?"

Son: "Dad, I'm sorry. I did the best I could."

Me: "Did you do the best you could? Because I know and you know you can do better than that."

Son: "Dad, I did study. There were questions on the test I didn't expect."

Me: "Well, if there were questions on the test you didn't expect, then that tells me you probably didn't study as much as you could have."

Son: "Dad, I'm SORRY!"

Whether my son needed to put more time into studying was the case or not, reacting like that didn't make the situation any better, it didn't improve his grades for the next test, and the likelihood he was going to tell me something he wasn't proud of the next time wasn't a high likelihood. In fact, conversations like this just drove more and more of a wedge between us.

I've learned over the years, and experts who are far smarter than I am have confirmed, that when our kids share something that they failed at or a challenge, what they need is safe place to land, where they can be guided through better questions to make their own conclusions.

Take that same situation (getting a D on the science test) and how I handle it now.

Me: "What was the most challenging part of your day?"

Son: "I got a D on the science test."

Me: "Oh man. Bummer. That probably doesn't feel good."

Son: "No, it doesn't."

Me: "Looking back on it, was there anything you would have done differently getting ready for the test?"

Son: "I guess I would have put some more time into studying for the test. I did study some. I thought it was enough, but there were questions on the test I didn't expect."

Me: "Yeah, that happens. Sometimes we think we did enough to prepare for something big, and then we get surprised because there were things we weren't expecting. You know, that even happens to me at work or sometimes during a podcast interview. If I don't prepare for the guest I am interviewing, the interview will go in a direction I didn't expect and perhaps not go the way I wanted."

Son: "Yeah, I guess that's what happened."

Me: "Tell me this, when is your next test?"

Son: "It's actually next Friday."

Me: "Cool. Based on the information you have, what would you do differently, getting ready for this next test?"

Son: "I would probably study more."

Me: "What days would you study, and how much time would you need?"

Son: "Umm…I would probably need to spend a little time each day Monday to Thursday. At least 30 to 45 minutes per night to get 100-percent ready."

Me: "Wow, I think that is a great plan! How can I support you? Do you need any help, or do you need me to just hold you to that?"

Son: "I think I will be good on my own, but you checking in on me on those nights would be helpful."

Me: "Of course! Let's both commit to it! I will check in on you when you come home, and then before bed, let me know how your studying went and if you need any additional help before we call it a night."

Son: "That sounds really good."

Me: "Awesome! Sounds like we have a plan. Proud of you for learning from this. Bad grades will happen, but it's more important we just keep learning from times when we fall short. That way, a shortfall can be a big learning moment. In life, you will have many of these that will happen. As long as we keep learning from shortfalls or mistakes, that is the main thing. Love you, man!"

Son: "Thanks, Dad! I appreciate you talking to me."

There were several elements of the above conversation that served to create psychological safety.

1. This whole conversation started with me asking the #2 question.
2. I responded with calm and with more questions.
3. I didn't shame or blame.
4. He felt safe telling me more information and the fact he didn't put in enough time into studying.
5. He stated what he learned and how he would be successful for the next test.
6. He created the structure for success for the next test.
7. He learned from his mistakes and articulated the lesson back to me.
8. We both felt really good about the conversation that could have otherwise gone in a very negative direction.
9. I didn't have to use shame, judgement, or blame to get the lesson to sink in. He articulated the lesson by answering the questions.
10. This type of conversation instills a growth mindset of learning.
11. This conversation elevates a relationship and bond with our kids.
12. This type of conversation increases the chances of my son coming to me with another situation he isn't proud of and seeking guidance.

The #2 question will increase the probability of our kids coming to us as teenagers when the stakes are higher. Perhaps our kids are tempted by drugs and alcohol. Maybe their friends are pressuring them to do something illegal. It could also be something really serious like suicidal thoughts. No matter what it is or how dark it could be, this question will create the environment that you are the safe place to land and come to for advice. My oldest boys are now 16 and 14 as I write this book. I can tell you this works! I'm shocked by the level of things they have shared with me. I don't say that to brag because at times, I don't even feel worthy of the trust they give me. I haven't always responded in the best way to their shortcomings and their mistakes. However, for the past several years, I have had thousands of conversations like the one above. I try to ask these questions every single day. These small deposits over time have built a level of trust and connection between us that I would have never thought possible.

QUESTION #3: "What are you most excited about tomorrow?"
Netflix has done a great job of hooking us into binge watching our favorite shows over the years. We can all relate to the times we have binged our favorite shows for five to eight hours at a time. We didn't even know how it happened. We just kept watching the next episode because of the hook point at the end of the last one.

This final question is your "Netflix Binge Hook Point" question. It's the "to be continued" question for the next day for your conversation to start back where you left it.

When we ask: "What are you most excited about tomorrow?", it puts our kids back into the state of gratitude and joy. They start thinking about what good is going to happen the next day instead of what they are dreading. With this question, we are guiding them to think about what is possible and what could be celebrated. Most adults we know are actually doing the opposite. We are focusing on what we are dreading for the next day or even week. We are looking at how we will get through or even get around something. That type of mentality puts us into surviving mode and not thriving mode. What we focus on will expand. If our kids (and us) focus on the negative and what we are dreading, that will expand. If we focus on possibilities and what we can create, that will expand as well.

This question also elevates the connection with our kids because they are, once again, bringing us to a high-point moment that excites them. When we share in high point moments that excite us, we give new energy and connection to a relationship. It's not a relationship that drains us. It's a relationship that brings us joy and fulfillment.

One of the coolest aspects of this question is that it's the "to be continued" aspect for the following day. When our kids state what they are most excited about for the following day, it gives us a high-level entry point to come back to the next day when we strike up a conversation.

Maybe our kids are excited about their cross-country meet. Perhaps they are excited about a presentation for their class they have been working hard on. It could be they are going to finally ask that girl to homecoming. It truly doesn't matter what it is; it only matters that it is important to them. When we ask how their meet went, their presentation for their class, or asking the girl to homecoming the next day, it shows we are deeply interested in their life. We are not only their father but also a trusted guide who wants to have a deep, meaningful connection with them. These are the bonds that create deep, meaningful human connection through trust, safety, and a bond.

If you commit to these three questions on a daily basis and use them properly, just watch how your relationship and your connection with your kids elevates. You might be thinking that these three questions are too easy and because they are too easy, they will never work. Their ease of use is actually what make them so elegant and effective. Get your reps in and use these questions every day.

Final Guidance for the Questions

Question #1: When your kids tell you about the best part of their day, don't simply move on to Question #2 without reflecting back what you heard. Reflect back with excitement and don't be afraid to ask for more detail. The more exciting detail that is shared, the BETTER! This question teaches our kids to dig into gratitude. When our kids share their gratitude with us, it elevates the energy, the connection, and the bond we have with our kids. It's pretty amazing to say the least.

Question #2: When your kids tell you about a low point, keep in mind they are being vulnerable with you. They are most likely sharing something with you they otherwise wouldn't unless you asked. They are also making snap judgments on whether or not they will tell you other difficult things depending on how you respond. Respond with a calm voice and be ready to guide (not lecture) through deeper questions so they articulate the lessons learned. This question will elevate the level of psychological safety our kids feel in the relationship. When we do this on a daily basis, it becomes easier for our kids to tell us the hard things they otherwise wouldn't.

Question #3: Reflect back with excitement and gratitude. Do not forget to ask about this the following day. When we follow up with something that was meaningful the next day, it shows we care and are interested. This question deepens the connection and relationships.

19 RAISING YOUNG MEN

> *"Every father should remember that one day his son will follow his example instead of his advice."*
>
> — Charles F. Kettering

When it comes to raising men, there are several elements that are important. In this chapter, we will get to a few of the most essential.

Raise a Young Man with Integrity

One of the most important aspects of raising a young man is teaching him to be a man of his word. The world is full of men who say one thing and do another. We all know them. We question their character and integrity. Over time, we stop trusting them.

When we keep our word to ourselves and others, we are building credibility. As men of our word, if we say we are going to do something, we do it. It's truly that simple, and there are several benefits to the practice of keeping our word.

First, we develop a higher level of self-trust. When we think of the word "trust," we usually think of trusting others or others trusting us. We immediately start thinking about trust that is external to the self. However, when we are true to our word, we develop a higher level of self-trust. In my humble opinion, your self-trust is more important than how much others trust you and vice versa, and, in fact, a high level of external trust actually starts with the foundation of self-trust. When we develop a high level of self-trust, we have higher levels of self-respect, self-worth, and integrity. If we trust ourselves more, we are more likely to trust others, and others are more likely to trust us.

Second, we can live a life with minimal regret or guilt. When we aren't true to our own word and the promises we have made to ourselves, we start to operate from a foundation of fear and guilt. Think of the promises you have made to yourself that you haven't fulfilled. If this is a pattern, over time, we begin to conclude that we cannot trust ourselves to stay true to our word. Conclusions about ourselves are deeper and more powerful than perceptions. We have all known people in our lives that are starters and not finishers with nearly every goal they set out to achieve. Overall, we don't trust those people, and they do not trust themselves. As a result, they live with a high level of regret and guilt. When we live this way, life doesn't feel fulfilling.

Third, people who are true to their word are extremely careful about what they commit to. People who say yes to everything rarely execute on everything they agree to. As a result, people can overcommit and become overwhelmed, burnt out, and defeated. We all know these people as well. They try to please everyone by being everything to everyone. In the end, they become nothing to everyone, even themselves.

The best way to teach young men to be men of their word is to be the living example of this way of life. Bottom line, if you make a promise to your wife or kids, keep it. If you say you will be somewhere at 7:00 p.m., show up at 6:50 p.m. If you schedule a date night with your son, keep it. If you say you are going to play basketball with your kids in the evening, do it.

Hold your kids accountable to their word, as well. Be a good accountability partner. It's easy for young men to let their promises go from time to time. Be willing to stand nose to nose and toes to toes with joyful accountability to ensure they execute.

Celebrate Honesty

Young men (and all human beings in general) can be tempted to lie. We lie because we want to avoid shame, blame, or pain. We view dishonesty as a potential easy road. Being honest can potentially require us to air out our dirty laundry. It can get us in trouble, and we might experience those above feelings—shame, blame, and guilt. At times, we can be brutal with our kids with punishments after they are honest about some wrongdoing. We come down hard and fast with consequences after they have come clean. I'm not saying that wrongdoing should go completely undisciplined, but when we blast our kids with guilt, shame, blame, and pain when they admit something, we are setting the stage for them to avoid coming to us when things matter most. Keep in mind, it takes courage to be honest when we are tempted to be dishonest. A lie is easier when we know we can get away with it. When your sons are honest in circumstances where lying is an option, celebrate the courage it took to be honest and link it to their integrity.

Believe it or not, we don't have to wait for these situations to arise. We can raise discussions with our kids that give them permission to tell the truth. We can ask our kids questions like:

- "What was something that challenged you today?"
- "What was something you failed at today that you are potentially afraid to tell me?"
- "What is something you would like to tell me that you think I might not understand?"
- "What is something you have done in the past that you aren't proud of?"

Any of these above questions will manufacture a solid conversation, and if my kids are honest with me and open up to me, they won't be met with discipline but rather discussion and curious inquiry to guide them towards making better decisions.

Recently, I asked one of these questions to my son. When I asked him, "What is something you have done in the past that you aren't proud of?", I saw him hesitate and take a deep breath. On this particular day, he had done something he knew was wrong and was so ashamed of.

During this season of our lives, we were traveling quite a bit as a family. As a result, I was pulling the kids out of school to travel with us. It wasn't a huge amount of time out of school, a few days here and there, but it was enough that he fell behind with his schoolwork. All of the boys have always been solid with getting decent grades, and we have never had any big issues with school, grades, or getting assignments done on time. None of my kids have ever really gotten in trouble at school for missing work or cheating. In hindsight, I pulled them out of school too much. They missed about six days of school over a 30-day time period. Not a lot of time, but over a full school week—enough to fall behind in a big way.

When I asked my son the above question, he crumbled with emotion and began to tell me about a situation that had happened earlier that day. He told me how behind he was with his work and how stressful it had become to catch up. He got nearly all of his assignments done but was really overwhelmed with one writing project in particular. He asked one of his friends for the answers to a few of the questions and was caught by his teacher. He was sent to the principal's office, and the consequence was detention after school the next day.

When he gave me all the detail of what had happened, he owned every single part of it. He didn't play the blame game. He knew what he had done was 100 percent wrong and he was willing to accept full responsibility. He told the teacher and the principal that what he did was wrong. He had no one to blame but himself. He didn't blame the time off. He didn't blame the teacher or even the work. The situation was what it was, and he knew he was wrong. He embraced the consequences to make it right.

When he told me, he was terrified I was going to lay down the hammer of more pain, guilt, shame, and additional consequences. However, that wasn't the approach that I took. We talked in depth about how wrong it is to cheat. We talked about the consequences in life and what happens to people who cheat and take the easy way out. In my mind, his dues were being paid by going to detention and not getting any credit for his assignment. I applauded his honesty and ownership. Every man will make mistakes, and a true man will own them. He will also embrace the consequences of his actions. There were no more lessons to teach. He learned. I am confident that I won't be facing this same situation with him in the future.

Now, I am sure some of you are reading this and thinking that I'm a softy or maybe I don't implement discipline in my house. Nothing is further from the truth. There are times, when wrongdoings are done, that there is disciplinary action that follows. However, for situations like this, it's more important that I help guide my children through problem-solving skills and learning from failure. If all I did was come down on my kids with blame, shame, and pain, they would be less likely to learn from their mistakes. Instead, by celebrating their honesty and asking them questions that help guide them to solutions, I can help them learn. I am also creating an environment where they can be authentic, vulnerable, and imperfect in front of their old man and it's a positive experience.

Here's another reason why it's important that honesty is celebrated. What I have learned from other men in our community who have kids older than me is that I can either create an environment where I am the first phone call when things go wrong, or I can create one where my kids never let me into their lives. Think of all the things that went wrong when you were growing up and potentially how terrified you were to tell your parents any of it. In fact, you most likely worked really hard to make sure they never found out. I'm in this fatherhood thing for the marathon, not the sprint. If my boys are at a party and they had too much to drink, I want them to pick up the phone and call me to get a ride without blame, shame, or pain. When their friends are doing drugs and they are getting peer pressured, I want them to feel welcome to come talk to me. When they are thinking about having sex for the first time, I want them to feel safe to come talk to me. When things go wrong in their lives, I want them to look to me as a guide that can help them navigate. I always encourage men to do 80 percent of the listening and simply ask questions that will help guide their kids to better outcomes. For the most part, lecturing doesn't work and it's not effective. After so much time of us being on our lecturing soapbox, kids will tune us out. On the flip side, if you engage them in conversation with solution-based questions, they are more likely to learn and follow through with their own plan of success.

A Man Is Kind but Formidable

For the majority of my childhood, I was overweight and bullied constantly. I was called names and physically beaten by other boys. I never defended myself. I would either run try to run away from it or just take it. I had no clue how to defend myself. I had no idea how to throw a punch or at least do something to get away. It was the most helpless feeling growing up. When this happens, you don't feel like a man because we believe that strong men can defend themselves.

When I got into high school, I found wrestling. Being real here, I wasn't very good my freshman year. I probably won three matches all year. I still joke to this day that I know what the ceilings on most gyms look like because I spend so much time on my back. However, when I came back my sophomore year for wrestling, I had lost some much-needed weight. I was more confident. I was more eager to learn. I viewed the wrestling skills I was learning as a way to not only get healthier but also an avenue to defend myself outside the wrestling room. During my sophomore year, I stopped allowing bullying to happen. I made a decision I was going to stand up for myself, even if I got beat. I felt more confident defending myself because I knew how. There were some battles I won and some I lost, but over time, people stopped messing with me. By my junior year, no one was bullying me any longer. I had lost weight. I was more confident. I was known as someone who wouldn't hesitate to fight back.

I look back on my time wrestling, and it was such a positive experience overall, even though it is one the toughest sports in youth athletics. It was good for my physical health because I was able to get fit and lose weight. It was good for my mental health because I felt more confident and I knew I had skills to defend myself when needed. After I graduated high school, I went into college seeking more martial arts skills. I found a Tae Kwon Do club and was a part of that for two years. After college, I continued with martial arts for another seven years, learning Kuk Sool Won. After Kuk Sool Won, I joined a Krav Maga studio with my oldest son, Ethan, who was 10 at the time. All four of my boys have had martial arts training over the years. As a matter of fact, my oldest and I are going to be doing Ju Jitsu in the near future.

I have always instilled in my boys that it is their right to defend themselves when threatened. It's also their right to defend their friends, family, and people they care about. My boys know what it means to be "sheepdog strong" in our house. The sheepdog is there to protect the sheep from the wolves. The wolves are the bullies and the people who want to do harm. The sheepdog isn't a wolf but will be a dangerous adversary to the wolf. My boys understand and identify with the sheepdog mentality.

Ethan, my oldest son, is very empathetic, compassionate, and gentle. He has never started a fight in his life. He has never bullied any other kid. In fact, there was a part of me for years that was worried if he could defend himself. For a long time growing up, he was a bit on the smaller side. He wasn't very interested in athletics. He loved music and playing instruments. Over the years, he has had very short stints with bullies trying to push him around. He has always done a good job of standing his ground in a non-violent fashion. He never got into any fight, no matter what had happened.

There was one day when Ethan was nine years old that he had to not just defend himself, but his younger brother Mason (nine years old at the time). There was a boy (11 years old as well), who was much bigger than both Ethan and Mason. The kid had a history of pushing others around and used his much bigger size to do so. At the time, Ethan was all of about 75 pounds, and the bully was well over 100 pounds. One day, Ethan, Mason, and the bully were playing with a group of other kids in the neighborhood. The bully had targeted Mason to take out some aggression and began pushing him around. All of this was happening right outside my house while I was working in my garage, so I got to see the whole thing go down. The bully started to get really aggressive and take Mason down when, out of nowhere, I saw Ethan unleash and defend his younger smaller brother. Ethan simply tackled the bigger kid to the ground to restrain him and stop him from coming after his baby bro. Upon the takedown, I saw the bully's father run out of his house and get in Ethan's face. It was obvious he only saw the tail end of what had happened. He didn't see his son, who had a history of being a bully, push Mason around. He immediately got nose to nose and toes to toes with Ethan and began yelling at him for tackling his son. As much as I wanted to intervene, I didn't. I purposely just watched to see what was going to play out and see how Ethan responded. Obviously, if the dad was going to hurt my son, I wouldn't have hesitated to step in. I didn't get the sense it was going in that direction. It was nothing more than a stern lecture on "how dare my son do that to his son."

Ethan came home devastated, and upon seeing me, he thought he was going to be in big trouble. He ran up to me crying and told me what happened. I had seen it go down. I knew what happened.

He was upset because he had to get physical but was also upset because he thought he would be in trouble. I reassured him that he wasn't in trouble. In fact, I was proud of him. In that situation, he was sheepdog strong. He got between a bigger kid, a bully, and his brother to protect him. He put himself in danger to protect his family. He was in no trouble with me. In fact, I reminded him what it meant to be sheepdog strong. I reminded him he has the right to defend himself and people he loves from threats.

We live in a dangerous world. Part of our duty as men is to protect ourselves and our family. Our job as fathers is to ensure our boys have the skills do so. I'm not a promoter of violence, but I am a believer that there are violent people in the world who desire to do harm to others. In the face of that evil, we must be ready to protect ourselves, our family, friends, and people we love.

Teach Them to Live Boldly and Fail Forward

Risk taking is not just something most young men avoid; it's something most human beings avoid. To add insult to injury, our generation of parents are known as the "helicopter parents." I get it. I was one with my two older boys. I didn't want to see them fall down, fail, or even feel the pain of failure. As adults we feel the pain of failure run extremely deep. We remember what it was like when we were younger and we got a failing grade on a test. We felt like failing that test was a personal failure. Perhaps we viewed ourselves as stupid or not good enough. It wasn't about the test; it was about how we failed as a human being. Think of a time you messed up badly growing up—maybe you messed up a big play in the game. You might have viewed that mess up as failing the whole team, your parents, and even yourself. This mentality impacts us big time throughout our lives and into adulthood. How many times have we passed up on taking a risk because we didn't want to deal with the feeling of failure? Perhaps you have a passion to launch a business venture, but you haven't done it because of the fear of failing.

When it comes to failure, many of us have a fixed mindset and not a growth mindset. Carol Dweck wrote an incredible book called *Mindset: The New Psychology of Success*. The book is an absolute game changer on many levels. The overall theme of the book is that human beings either operate with a growth mindset or a fixed mindset.[12]

Fixed mindset: "In a fixed mindset, people believe their basic qualities, like their intelligence or talent, are simply fixed traits. They spend their time documenting their intelligence or talent instead of developing them. They also believe that talent alone creates success—without effort."

Growth mindset: "In a growth mindset, people believe that their most basic abilities can be developed through dedication and hard work—brains and talent are just the starting point. This view creates a love of learning and a resilience that is essential for great accomplishment."

If we operate with a growth mindset, we are more welcoming of failing forward because we are eager to learn the lessons within the journey. We aren't nearly as attached to the outcome and won't label ourselves as a "success" or "failure" based on the situational outcome.

When it comes to a fixed mindset, there are several less-than-desirable characteristics that can be observed.

---

[12]. Carol Dweck, *Mindset: The New Psychology of Success*, New York: Random House, 2006.

1. A person with a fixed mindset believes that all of our talents and traits are fixed and determined for life. They believe there is no growth, only success and failure.

2. A person with a fixed mindset avoids risks as all costs. They are uber focused on not failing. As a result, these people never take any risks in life.

3. A person with a fixed mindset believes that effort is for those who simply aren't smart enough. They don't believe in preparing for a test or presentation because they think the effort is meaningless. It's only about the outcome.

4. A fixed mindset covers this person's flaws, and they will get defensive if you point out something as a potential weakness. These people are rarely coachable because they view feedback as a personal attack.

5. A person with a fixed mindset is threatened by the success of others. This individual hates seeing others succeed because they view others' successes as a reminder of how they are failing.

We all know people in our lives that operate with at least some of these traits. Obviously, these traits are not associated with success. In fact, these traits will keep us from our greatness. On the other hand, a growth mindset will help us to achieve greatness. The characteristics of a growth mindset are listed below.

1. People with a growth mindset have higher confidence and self-belief. They look at life and situations as a way to grow and evolve. They don't buy into the belief that they are labeled by the end result. They move forward in situations, looking

to grow, evolve, and overcome obstacles that come their way. They believe in themselves more because they have track record of taking risks and overcoming adversity.

2. People with a growth mindset take calculated risks, which are different from careless risks. People with a growth mindset don't go about situations blindly. They think about their decisions but don't overanalyze every detail to the point of paralysis. They carefully weigh the pros and cons and move forward in a calculated fashion.

3. People with a growth mindset don't allow past failures to hold them back from potential future success, knowing that failure and learning are part of the process. They view their failures as lessons. As a result, they use these lessons as a way to make calculated decisions for the future.

4. People with a growth mindset are more resilient, simply because they've put in the reps in the past. We all face adversity and setbacks. The difference with growth-mindset individuals is that they have simply had more failures and setbacks in their journey. As a result, they are more accustomed to adversity, which makes them more resilient.

5. Growth-mindset individuals surround themselves with more positive people. We all know the sayings, "We are who we hang with" and "We are the average of the five people we spend the most time with." When it comes to their circle of friends, people with a growth mindset put positive friendships with growth and support at the helm.

My wife and I teach a growth mindset to our sons by being the example and guide. If they see us terrified of taking risks because of looming mistakes, they will follow suit. If they see us not growing ourselves, they will follow suit.

On December 31, 2021, my 14-year-old son, Mason, challenged me to joining him on a journey that definitely terrified me at first. Mason's birthday is January 1, 2008. We have had the same tradition for his birthday for years, hosting a New Year's Eve party at our house. Jessica and I have friends over. The boys have friends over. We order food, snacks, drinks, and birthday cake. We serve Mason's birthday cake at midnight on January 1, and as he blows out his candles and we celebrate, we also talk about what big things we are going to do as a family for the upcoming year.

On this particular celebration, Mason told me that he had a dream and a goal to compete in a teen bodybuilding show on April 30, 2022. As I looked at him completely stunned, I quickly did the math and realized this was 16 weeks away. As I sat there eating junk food and beer, he looked at me and told me he wanted me to do this with him. At first, my fixed mindset crept in. I began to think about my age. *I'm 46 years old. Aren't I too old for something like this? What if I can't get ready in time and look like an idiot on stage? What if I don't make Mason proud?*

Then, I began to think about the possibilities. I started thinking about what the 16-week journey could look like for us. I thought about all the quality time we would spend at the gym. I thought about the conversations we would share. I reflected upon how we would grow together as father and son going through something insanely difficult. Instead of thinking of the journey with "a result-only focus," I embraced the growth that was associated with the experience of doing this together.

Over the course of the 16 weeks, we trained over 200 hours together and achieved some amazing milestones. I went from 194 pounds and 17 percent body fat to 165 pounds and down to about 7 percent body fat. The diet was grueling, and some of the sessions at the gym were exhausting, but I loved the fact we were doing this together. Mason also achieved many amazing milestones. He put on about seven pounds of muscle, lost some serious body fat, and trained extremely hard. The beautiful thing that came out of this 16 weeks of prep was the impact on our growth as individuals. We learned more about our own self-discipline, work ethic, and supporting each other through the process. We embraced the journey and not the outcome of what place we got at the show.

We had several conversations throughout the 16-week training, but one conversation in particular stands out as the best of all. In the last week of our prep, we were in the gym, working legs for the last time before the show, which was only five days away. I asked him, "What has kept you going this whole time? I've seen you train every day, even when you were tired. I saw you turn away junk food when I know it was insanely hard for you. I've seen you sacrifice more in the past 16 weeks than in your entire life. What has kept you going, and what have you learned?" His answer blew my mind. It was so powerful and a lesson that will serve him his entire life. It was a response that I would have never thought to hear from a 14-year-old young man.

He said, "I've learned determination over motivation." His response really intrigued me, so I asked him to explain it.

He went on, "I've learned that motivation will come and go. There have definitely been times during this 16-week process that I haven't been motivated. In fact, there have been times when it has gotten really hard. I was determined to finish this process from the very start. Knowing that I was determined to finish no matter what made the decision to keep going, even when I wasn't motivated to do so, a very easy decision."

I will never forget him sharing that. It was so powerful. It took me by such surprise to hear a 14-year-old young man reflect upon such a powerful life lesson. In that moment, I hugged him. I told him that this lesson would serve him for the rest of his life. There will be many things that he will do and many things he will not be motivated to do. Determination over motivation is a powerful lesson that we only learn through going through something that forces us to grow.

The outcome of the show was everything we could have both hoped for! Mason ended up taking second place in two different divisions. He also won one of the most coveted awards for a physique competitor, best presentation. The award for best presentation usually goes to a competitor who has been in the bodybuilding competition game for a long time. They present themselves, their physique, and their routine the best. I have never seen a show where a teen, and the youngest person in the whole show, won that award. It didn't happen by accident. I saw Mason perfect his routine every single day over and over. He wanted it to be perfect. He worked incredibly hard, and getting that award was such a high point for him as well. Dear old dad didn't do so bad either. I won second in two different divisions and fourth in another division. For me the awards and the placements were a bonus. In my mind, I had already won everything that was meaningful to me. For me, it was having 200 hours of one-on-one time with Mason over 16 weeks of prep. It was the conversations we had. It was the pain we shared. It was how we held each other accountable. To me that was the win! I gave my medals to my two younger sons. They are a symbol of hard work and a way to remember the day, but for me, the real award was the time with Mason. I will go to my grave remembering all of it.

Many of us will only do something like this and be focused solely on the outcome. If the outcome is potentially less than desirable or if there is risk we won't succeed, many of us won't take the journey. If we have a growth mindset, the results are important, but what is more important are the amazing life lessons and growth that emerges.

When it comes to raising our sons, living boldly with a growth mindset is a powerful life lesson. As we enter into a journey of any kind, we can be open to the life lessons and the growth that emerges instead of being 100-percent focused on the "pass or fail outcome."

Connecting with Our Sons Through Activity

Many of us want to connect with our boys through conversations. This is never a bad way to go, but it isn't the only way to go. Young boys connect with other men (even their dads) through experiences, activities, fun, and play. Think about it. As men, we have some of our best connections while doing things like playing golf, fishing, camping, exercising, hunting, shooting firearms, doing martial arts, or even learning a new skill. Experiences and activities create a bond with other men. They create a shared experience that is beneficial to each individual.

Reflect on some of your experiences with your own dad growing up. Did you play catch? Did your dad maybe teach you how to hit a ball? Did he teach you something like changing the oil in your car or changing a tire? We look back on times like those and usually remember the joy and positivity it brought us.

Now that we are raising our own sons, I can tell you that nothing has changed when it comes to the bonds that are formed through doing a shared activity. Over the past several years of raising four boys, some of the best conversations, connections, and memories were made while we were doing a shared activity. I have taken the boys fishing, camping, hiking, rock climbing, traveling to new cities/places, learning something new (like how to put up a backsplash in your kitchen), playing catch, martial arts, learning firearms safety, etc. All of these activities have provided more depth to the relationship. Doing activities together create memories and deeper bonds.

Young boys have a desire to be adventurous and try new things. One of the greatest gifts we can give them as fathers is to go on adventures with them and take them on ours. Some of the best conversations I have had are with my boys on hikes, fishing, and camping. We talk in depth about their world, challenges they go through, girls, friendships, and life in general.

Conversations are great, but if we really want to provide depth in the relationship, doing activities together create so many benefits.

Rites of Passage for Young Men

We currently live in a period of time where rites of passages for young boys have completely gone away. We live in a society where some young boys have no clue what it means to be a man—the basic skills that young boys learn at a foundational level about who they are and becoming a good leader.

Over the past several years, I have taken my two oldest boys (Ethan 16 and Mason 14) on two different rites of passage.

The first rite of passage I took my boys on was when Ethan was 13 and Mason was 11. I hosted a Dad Edge Mastermind retreat for 12 men in the mountains of Breckenridge, Colorado for a weekend. I secured a large Airbnb that slept 18 people in the middle of the Rocky Mountains. There was barely cell service to be had. My boys, the participants, and I spent three days in the mountains.

The first day we masterminded all day (my boys included). The second day was dedicated to successfully summiting a 14er called Mt. Quandary (14,165 ft), which was a 12-hour round-trip hike to the top and back. The third day was a half day of masterminding and travel back home.

I brought both Ethan and Mason on this trip for two distinct reasons. First, I wanted the boys to experience firsthand what good-quality iron-sharpens-iron friendships look like. The participants who were a part of this in-person retreat are amazing men. These men are eager to learn from each other, treat each other with respect, and have each other's best interests at heart. Many of us will go a lifetime and never experience high-quality friendships. I wanted the boys to experience this firsthand so they could measure every friendship they have in their lives against what they saw at this retreat. Secondly, I also made this trip a rite-of-passage experience for both of the boys. Hiking up a 14er is no easy task. It's an accomplishment that many never attempt. So, I took it as an opportunity for both of them to experience. They were both able and very willing.

We all woke up on the second day at 3:30 a.m. to conquer the mountain. Unfortunately, Ethan woke up with some pretty bad altitude sickness. He felt a bit dizzy, tired, and had a headache. Luckily, I also hired a guide who was a paramedic, and he suggested that Ethan stay back at the house and not do the climb. It was a tough decision, but it was definitely the right one. Ethan ended up staying back and recovered from the altitude sickness. Mason, on the other hand, was feeling fine and was ready to dominate the mountain.

We started on the trailhead around 4:30 a.m. Upon the start of the hike, I told Mason we would be stopping several times along the way to enjoy the views and to talk about new ways of living, going from a young boy to a young man. I wrote him a letter that included seven pillars of becoming a young man that I read to him along the way and finished the remainder upon the top of the summit. I've included that letter at the end of the book so you have a copy.

The hike up Mt. Quandary symbolized the final steps of his boyhood journey. The summit of the mountain symbolized the peak and end of his journey as a boy in this life. The summit down the mountain symbolized the first steps into his journey to life as a young man. Since I have included the letter in the back, I won't go into all the detail of the seven pillars now. However, I will share a story that really hits home why this trip was a perfect example of this rite of passage.

If you have never summited a 14er, it's not for the faint of heart. The hike can be exhausting and long. The air is thin at 14,000 feet, which makes it more difficult to breathe. The hike can be challenging for even the fittest people if you aren't used to it. Both of us started the hike with all the right gear and supplies. We each had a CamelBak full of water, a backpack full of dried fruit, nuts, beef jerky, electrolytes, Gatorade, rain gear, extra socks, and extra clothes. I was easily carrying 20 pounds on my back, and Mason had about 10 on his. Ten extra pounds is a lot when you weigh only 80 pounds.

Mason is a very athletic young man. He has a solid foundation in sports like football and wrestling. So, he was used to physically pushing himself. When we started the hike, he was all smiles. Even several hours into the hike, he was going strong. It was about 10:30 a.m. (six hours into the hike) when I noticed he was getting a bit weary and tired. He was in front of me, and I kept noticing he was getting just a bit wobbly as he we ascended in altitude. We were about 90 minutes from the summit when I really started seeing some fatigue set in with him.

Upon one of our breaks, I told him that I noticed he was getting tired and for safety reasons, he should give me his backpack full of food, extra water, clothes, and rain gear so I could carry it for him for a while. He wasn't having any of that. Mason is the type of young man who never backs down from a challenge and certainly doesn't want anyone to carry his load for him. He views that as a sign of weakness. After he refused, I encouraged him to give up his bag because I was concerned about him safely making it to the top. He refused again. At this point, I had to play the "dad card," meaning I demanded that he take off his backpack so I could carry it for him. I told him it was no longer a request; it was an order. He reluctantly took off his backpack and handed it over for me to carry. His head hung low as I took his bag and threw it over my shoulder. He looked defeated and even ashamed.

I put the backpack on top of my own and secured it on my back and shoulders. At this point, I was now carrying my own CamelBak, my backpack, and his on my back. It wasn't the most comfortable way to go, but it was better than watching my fatigued 11-year-old son under the burden of the weight on his shoulders.

He turned around and began leading our group back up the mountain. His head hung low at the ground. His pace was a bit slower, and he was displaying all the signs of shame and defeat. I walked up beside him and began to walk side-by-side with him. I put my arm around him and poured into him a bit.

I said, "Mason, I know you are upset about giving up your bag. I get it. I'm sure you feel like it's only out of weakness that you gave up your bag. It's never weakness to ask for help when we need it. I just want you to be safe. Who knows, maybe on this hike I might need your help!"

He responded saying: "I know, Dad. I just didn't want the help. I wanted to do it all on my own."

I said, "I know, son, but at times, every man needs some help. Again, maybe before this hike is done, you will be helping me."

Looking back on that conversation, I most likely came across as condescending. I honestly didn't think I would need the help of my 11-year-old son. After all, I had done 14ers before and I prided myself on always being physically fit enough to do just about anything. I was wrong. I would have never predicted the humility and lessons I learned from my Mason on that hike until we started our way down the mountain.

We ended up summiting the top of Mt. Quandary just past noon on that day. It took us nearly eight hours to get to the top. We made it with seven of the twelve original men. Four of the men made it halfway and decided it was a bit much. So, they headed back. One of the men never even made it out of the Airbnb because of his own altitude sickness. When we got to the top of the mountain, we ate some lunch, took some amazing photos of the breathtaking view, and I read Mason the remainder of the letter I wrote him. It was such an emotional experience for both of us. Upon hearing my letter, he broke down crying. Upon seeing him cry, I started to cry. He told me the letter and the experience meant so much to him. It would be something he would remember for the rest of his life.

After we celebrated, got all our photos, and cried out all our tears, we decided it was time to get down the mountain. We were only about 10 minutes down the mountain (with about four hours to go) when I suddenly felt my quads completely lock up. Both of my quads started to cramp so badly that I could tell I might be in serious trouble. They started locking up to the point that the pain started to radiate down my legs and even into my lower back. At first, I tried to ignore the pain and thought if I didn't focus on it, it might just go away on its own if I kept moving. Unfortunately, that didn't work. I suddenly had to stop. I told Mason that I needed a minute to stretch my legs because they were locking up. I took both backpacks and my CamelBak off and began to stretch out my legs. After about 10 minutes, the cramps went away. I downed about 20 ounces of water, put my CamelBak and the backpacks back on, and started making my way down the mountain.

About 20 more minutes into the decent, my legs locked up again. This time it was more severe and more intense. I stopped and ripped everything off my back. I got on the ground and started stretching aggressively, but nothing was working. I looked at Mason as I started stretching, and he looked really concerned. Up to this point, he had never really seen me in a weakened state. The pain from my quads was unreal, and I couldn't get the cramps out no matter how aggressively I was stretching. I thought I was in big trouble. *How in the world am I going to get down this mountain if I can't move my legs?* I started thinking about the worst-case scenario and being airlifted off the mountain. I couldn't imagine the trip ending like that, especially since Mason and I had so many amazing moments. Our guide/paramedic told me that I needed electrolytes in a bad way. I started slamming bottles of Gatorade and eating beef jerky and bananas. After about 30 minutes of stretching, rehydrating, and taking in some salt and potassium, the cramps had subsided.

I felt relieved because I was pretty certain the cramps were gone for good. I stood up and put my CamelBak on. I started looking all over the place for my backpack and Mason's so I could put those on as well. The odd thing was, they were nowhere to be found. I looked over at Mason and couldn't believe what I was seeing. He had his CamelBak on along with his backpack and mine. I was in shock. It looked unbelievably uncomfortable. After all, my

80-pound son was now carrying about 20 pounds on his back! I went over to him and demanded that he take off both bags and give them to me. He refused. I demanded again. He refused again.

What happened next I will never forget. He looked at me dead in the eye and said, "You told me that there might be a time on this hike where you needed my help like I needed your help. You told me that part of being a man is being brave enough to ask and accept help when we need it most. I would like to help you now."

With tears and my eyes and every part of me wanting to disagree with him, I just hugged him. This was a beautiful moment for him, and I wasn't going to take that away. I decided to let him carry my backpack for as long as he wanted or at least as long as it was safe. For the next two hours down the mountain, he led us and traversed the decent with over 20 pounds on his back. For the longest time, I had imagined the beautiful memories and moments we would create on that mountain, but I would have never bet on that moment. I was (and still am) so proud of him. Part of his rite of passage, in addition to all the life lessons we talked about on the way up, at the top, and the way down, was this amazing moment of him helping his old man when I was in a vulnerable state.

Over the course of that 12-hour journey, my son had hiked up that mountain a little boy and descended a young man. The experience of the mountain, the hike, the scenery, the letter about the seven pillars of manhood, and the descent down the mountain will be forever cemented into our fondest memories.

Perhaps you are wondering if my oldest son, Ethan, ever went on the same quest as Mason. Once we got back home, Ethan couldn't let go of the fact that his brother conquered the mountain and he didn't. He talked about how much it bothered him that he couldn't conquer the mountain every day. So, I booked a trip for three weeks later, and we conquered Mt. Bierstadt. Mt. Bierstadt is a well-known 14er in Idaho Springs, Colorado. It was a very similar trip to the one with Mason, and perhaps even sweeter for Ethan because it was a journey that he and I got to do one on one.

Rites of Passage for Fathers AND Sons

I enjoyed conquering the 14ers with both of my boys, but to be honest, I didn't know exactly what I was doing when I took my boys on those hikes. I was never taken through a rite of passage growing up and definitely didn't know everything that should be involved. So, over the years, I have looked deeper into rites of passages for not only boys but for fathers as well.

In 2021, I met a good friend and mentor by the name of Bedros Kuelien. Bedros has an amazing story—a self-made entrepreneur who escaped communism to come to the United States when he was just a kid. A true rags-to-riches story, no doubt.

Bedros is a best-selling author, speaker and business consultant. He's the founder and CEO of Fit Body Boot Camp, one of the nation's fastest growing franchises, and an investor in over a dozen companies, ranging from subscription software platforms to digital ad agencies and even mastermind and coaching services.

He's known as the hidden genius that entrepreneurs, best-selling authors, and thought leaders turn to when they want to create high-level mastermind and coaching programs, quickly scale their businesses, and solve their most pressing bottlenecks so that they can make the quantum leap to massive success.

He is also most known for being the founder of the Modern Day Knight program. The project is a 75-hour self-development program for men who want to break free from the lower version of themselves. It is a physical, mental, and even emotional crucible that helps men shatter self-doubt, gain clarity on their life's work, heal from trauma, and help level up their mindset, money, and meaning of life. It's not an experience for the faint of heart and has about a 50 percent dropout rate.

Bedros is also known for being the founder of the Squire Program. The Squire is a 15-hour father/son journey that is taken together. The Squire is designed to help teach a young man how to operate and lead in life through confidence, integrity, and character. The program also teaches fathers how to continually instill these qualities into their sons to make them great leaders and protectors.

In January of 2022, Ethan and I signed up for Squire – class 004. I am not at liberty to talk about the details that transpire at the Squire, but what I can tell you is that the experience was absolutely life changing for both Ethan and me. The 15-hour event was filled with physical, mental, and emotional testing. It wasn't a beat down by any means, but it also wasn't easy. There were five instructors, including Bedros, who led the entire group throughout the day. The other instructors came from various backgrounds and included a former Navy SEAL, a former US Marine, a former SWAT officer, and even a professional MMA fighter/chaplain.

The entire day was filled with tests and evolutions that tested our communication and leadership skills. The evolutions revealed some of our greatest strengths and also some of our underlying weaknesses. Overall, each evolution taught both father and son game-changing lessons in leadership, manhood, and communication. When we completed a physically challenging evolution with our sons and the other participants, the instructors were always fantastic about bringing us together for genuine coaching moments so we could take these lessons back to the real world.

It was an experience that Ethan and I will take to our deathbeds. We learned a lot about ourselves and each other through the process. It has become a foundational experience that we reference a lot in our conversations. When he talks to me about peer pressure or things that his friends are getting into, we refer back to the lessons learned at the Squire and lean heavily on them. We refer back to the coaching moments from the instructors for guidance on how to operate in life with character and integrity, even when the crowd doesn't. When Ethan is faced with the choice to stay disciplined with his schoolwork or working hard in sports, we refer back to the beautiful lessons we learned about hard work.

As a father, it gave me a solid template for how to better lead my son. I now have several lessons learned and experiences from that event that I bring up in conversation between the two of us. I will be taking my other three boys through this program when the times comes in the future.

Even though I cannot publicly share distinct details of the Squire, I did want to share the 30 Rules to live a life of impact and fulfillment that we learned.

1. When you make a promise, KEEP IT.
2. Audit your circle of friends. If they are losers and no longer align with your values, cut them out of your life.
3. Check your self-talk. The conversation you have with yourself today has the biggest influence on who you become tomorrow.
4. Stop wasting time. It's finite, and you're running out of it.
5. Money is a vehicle to freedom and a tool like any other.
6. Stop being needy, seeking validation, and looking for approval from everyone.
7. Don't share your plans with the world. Show them instead.
8. Suffer, challenge yourself, get uncomfortable, and lean into adversity. It's the fastest way to discover the next and highest version of yourself.

9. The greatest investment that can be made is the investment you make in your personal growth. Pour into self-development—that's where you'll get the highest return on investment.
10. Wake up when all your friends and peers are still asleep and start stacking wins.
11. Establish a morning routine based on discipline and structure.
12. You're a man, and men protect, provide, and stay prepared.
13. Eat clean, train hard, and stay lean and battle ready.
14. Talk less and ask more questions.
15. Write down your goals. Be specific. Read them daily and act on them with violent urgency and enthusiasm.
16. Sometimes it's not what you ADD to your life that makes a difference but what you REMOVE that counts.
17. Be kind. Don't be mean or a jerk.
18. Always be prepared to bring the violence in defense of yourself and others.
19. Leadership is always the problem; leadership is always the solution. Level up and lead.
20. Ego is your enemy. It creates blind spots and gives you an emotional limp.
21. Show respect to others and demand respect back through your words and actions.
22. The more complex problems you can solve, the more money you will make. When you make money, invest it and be generous with it.

23. Establish your core values and moral character and hold yourself accountable to them.
24. Always maintain emotional discipline. Weak men react; strong men respond.
25. No matter the job, do it well. Your reputation is built and destroyed with every job you do.
26. In any task, there are two things that are 100 percent in your control: effort and attitude.
27. Create peace. Seek out peace. But be prepared to bring violence when violence is the only option.
28. Step into the gap and stand up for those who can't stand up for themselves.
29. Never negotiate your goals and dreams.
30. In life there's only one person you will choose, your wife. Make the right choice.

The world as know it is starving for good men. We need more fathers who are hungry and eager to embrace the challenge of raising good young men. We obviously live in a world where temptations for addictions, distractions, and vices are at every turn. Our sons want us to lead them. Our sons want us to step up as protectors, leaders, and providers. We must be willing and able to answer that call.

20 RAISING YOUNG WOMEN

> *"When a father gives his daughter an emotional visa to strike out on her own, he is always with her. Such a daughter has her encouraging, understanding daddy in her head, cheering her on—not simply as a woman but as a whole, unique human being with unlimited possibilities."*
>
> — Victoria Secunda

You Will Be the First Man in Her Life

I am blessed to have world-class coaches who work for me in The Dad Edge Alliance. There is one man in particular, Chris Barry, who is not only an amazing coach for men but also the father to four daughters. Over the past several years, I have seen Chris do amazing things with his daughters to show them how a good man operates. He goes above and beyond to not just teach them but also show them. He believes that part of his job as a father to his daughters is to set the bar extremely high so that his girls will expect other men to do the same. If they aren't setting the bar as high as dad, most likely they will not make the cut as a life partner.

Chris has had this amazing tradition of taking his daughters out on dates ever since they were little. He truly goes all out. When I say he truly goes all out, I am not talking about a five-star restaurant with gifts and spoils. What I mean is that he goes all out on the experience of the evening. He is all about the attention to detail—the small things that truly matter.

He tells his daughters what time to be ready on the night of their date and what time he will be picking them up. He also suggests what they should wear if they are going to do something fancy or if it's more casual and active.

He ensures that he is on time for the date. He is never late because not being on time means that he isn't true to his word. If he says he will be there at 6:00 p.m. to pick her up, he is there by 5:55 p.m. When he picks her up, he has been known to greet her with a flower and even a flower for her mom (his wife). He is sure to compliment her on outfit in a truly respectful way. He tells her mom where they will be, what they will be doing, and asks if the time they arrive back home is acceptable.

When he leaves with his daughter, he holds the door open for her and takes her hand as she steps down off the porch. He will then lead her to the passenger side of the car and open the door for her. On the way to the restaurant, he will ask her good questions that help create connection. He approaches her with genuine curiosity and appreciation. To him, the evening is an adventure of connection, good conversation, and learning about her.

Once they arrive to their date, he exits the car and tells her he will get her door. He walks around to the passenger side of the car and opens the car door for her, followed by her hand in his as he helps her out of the car. When they arrive at their date destination (call it dinner for this example), he will lead her to her table and pull the chair out for her before she sits. He sits down face to face with her and begins asking in-depth, generative questions to learn more about her. He asks her things like:

1. What has been your favorite memory growing up, and why is it so meaningful?
2. What are things that I do that make you feel most loved, most seen, and most heard?
3. Where do you see yourself in five years?
4. If you could do your dream job, what would it be?
5. If you could travel anywhere and bring anyone, where would you go, and who would you bring with you?
6. What have been some of the best life lessons you have learned from your parents?
7. Who is your best friend, and what personality qualities to you love most about them?

The evening is filled with great conversation. Chris is not only intentional with his questions but also reflects back and validates when she answers. Every question is meant to be a conversation starter and not a rapid-fire interview. If she gets up to use the restroom during the meal, he stands as she does out of respect. At the end of the dinner, he pulls her chair out for her. He leads her to the car where he will open her door for her again. On the way home, he shares how much he enjoyed getting to know the person she is and the conversation. He also praises and appreciates her for some of the things that really resonated with him. At the end of the evening, he walks her to the door and hugs her. He asks permission to schedule another date night if she is willing to do so.

Chris is no stranger to chivalry. His goal is the set the bar extremely high so his daughters have zero tolerance for anything less. Personally, I love this approach to raising daughters. This type of experience for both dad and daughter is extremely powerful.

For her, she gets one-on-one time with her dad. She gets to experience a real man with real manners. She also gets to experience a man who is attentive, present, and genuinely interested in the person she is. She gets to experience a man with high-level conversation skills. She experiences the feeling of feeling safe on a date.

For him, he gets to share one-on-one time with his daughter. Through the intentional conversation he gets to know more about her past, present, and even dreams of the future. He gets to know her heart. He also gets to set the stage and the expectations for the men that will come in and out of her life. She will always compare an incredible experience like this to every man who comes her way. This type of connection is second to none.

Never forget that you are the first man in her life. She will compare all men who come into her life against the standards that you set.

She Will Also Learn How to Be Loved by How You Love Her Mom

We covered this in a previous chapter, but the same rules apply here. The best lessons are caught and not taught. We can teach our daughters how a functional marriage works, but it's more important to just show them. Keep in mind, she has a front-row seat to the relationship you have with her mom. She is watching every move you make whether you think so or not. It's difficult to teach what an extraordinary marriage looks like unless we are willing to live it.

Be mindful of how you communicate with your wife. Treat her with respect and use kind words. Don't name call, bash, or be disrespectful. If she sees you doing this, her standards for how men treat her will follow suit as she gets older.

Be affectionate with your wife in front of her. Obviously, there are boundaries relative to the level of affection we show in front of our kids in general, but don't be afraid to hug your wife, kiss her, and hold her hand.

Ask your wife generative questions in front of your daughter to show that you are constantly courting and curious about her. When your daughter sees her dad never getting lazy when it comes to courting his wife, she won't settle for anything less.

Lead your wife in an empowering way and be collaborative with decisions. Let your daughter see you collaborating with your wife by making choices and helping her make choices. Don't be the guy who sits back and never has skin in the game for big or little decisions.

Love your wife in her love language and be public about it in front of your daughter. If your wife's love languages are words of affirmation, compliment your wife in front of her. Let your daughter know that you know mom feels most loved when she is seen, appreciated, and complimented. When she sees that you not only know this and live it, she won't settle for a man who is anything less.

When your wife speaks to you, listen for what she is feeling and validate her. The world is filled with men who simply want to fix their wives instead of listening. By now we all know that is not what our wives want most of the time. Take the time to listen and validate your wife's feelings in front of your daughter so she sees how a real man listens.

Teach Your Daughter How to Stay Safe Through Play

Back in November of 2019, I had the honor of interviewing Emily McCarthy on *The Dad Edge Podcast*. Emily spent several years as a CIA case officer and she actually had to get clearance to be able to talk on my show. She made it well known that she couldn't talk or give any details about her time with the CIA, which was fine for the interview because what I really wanted to vet out was the impact her dad had on her life growing up. Emily is the gold standard of a confident, strong woman who is also genuine and empathetic—a very rare combination of personality traits for any person, male or female. She is also the co-founder of GORUCK.

When she came on the show, she shared several stories of the impact her father had on her and the lessons he taught her. While I am going to share a couple of stories here, the bottom line of her experience with her dad growing up was that he was always there and always available.

Emily grew up in Jacksonville, Florida with her mom, dad, and younger brother. Her mom was a teacher, and her dad was a mortgage broker. Emily shared that she learned how to protect herself and be prepared from her dad, who did it through play. She mentioned that she would play hide and seek with her dad, brother, and even cousins. With a smile her dad would instruct her to hide in a place where he would never find her. That's exactly what she did. After he gave up looking for her, she revealed where she was hiding with a big smile on her face. Smiling back at her, he applauded her efforts to hide so well that he couldn't find her. He used this as a teaching moment. He instructed her that if anyone ever broke into the house or if she needed to hide from an intruder, she was to go to that same spot and hide until he came and got her. She mentioned that she loved games like this with him because he would always play but somehow include a teaching moment within the playtime. The older she got, the more she appreciated this about him.

Another story she shared was that for Christmas, her dad got both her brother and her a pair of boxing gloves. At the time the family were big fans of the sport, and it was something they all enjoyed watching. She mentioned that her and her brother would put on the gloves on their back porch while her dad taught them how to throw a punch and defend themselves. The approach he used was laughter and fun, but he also made sure they learned the skills. It wasn't that her dad was pro-violence, but he did want his son and daughter to have basic skills to defend themselves if needed.

Emily went on to tell a story about trying out for her seventh-grade basketball team in middle school. She was an excellent basketball player and loved the sport. She was one of the few seventh graders trying out for the team, as most of the team was made up of bigger, older eighth graders who had played on the team the year before. Emily did extremely well in tryouts. In fact, she did so well the first day of tryouts that the eighth-grade first-string players felt threatened that their position might be in jeopardy for the season due to her making the team. After the tryouts, Emily went into the locker room to change, where she found herself surrounded by five of the eighth-grade starters. They all banded together, forcing her up against the locker, and pinned her down. They threatened her and told her to not come back for the next day's tryouts. If she did return the next day, she was sure to get a beat down.

She came home and told her dad. She thought her dad might let her off the hook and be understanding as to why she wasn't going back the next day. She was in tears. Her dad was there to listen and comfort her, and he was also bold with what he thought her next steps should be.

He told her, "You are going back tomorrow. You are going to make the team and you are going to be starting for the team. Don't allow others who are threatened by you keep you from your dreams. Stand up and fight for what you want regardless of who is trying to stop you."

She was terrified, but she did just that. The next day, she showed up to tryouts. She was terrified, but making the team was extremely important to her. She looked up in the stands of the gymnasium, and there was her dad, in his work suit, watching her every move. He never went up and talked to the coaches and never interacted with the players. He was simply there. Knowing that her dad was there gave her the confidence to fight for what she wanted regardless of the fear of getting beaten up in the locker room. She ended up making the team, starting for the team, and the girls who bullied her became some of her closest friends. Looking back, she told me she knew full well that her dad probably rearranged his whole workday so he could be there. He never told her he was going to show up; he just did it. This gave her the courage to follow through. At times, daughters just need to know that their dad and their protector is present. He doesn't have to get directly involved with the fight; just being present is enough.

Emily shared there were many beautiful lessons that came out of that experience. She found bravery, and her dad believed in her. She is also grateful that her dad didn't let her off the hook to keep pursuing what she wanted. Now that she is a busy parent herself, she has immense gratitude for her dad just simply showing up and making his presence known.

As stated above, Emily went on to succeed in so many aspects of life. She attributes much of what she has learned about confidence, bravery, and even tough love to her dad.

At times, we want to simply rescue our daughters from danger. At times, we might even be apprehensive about teaching our daughters how to protect themselves. One of the best lessons that Emily's dad has taught us is that we can make life lessons like this fun and exciting. He also taught us the importance of showing up and making our presence known. The final lesson was to be able to stand up and fight for our dreams, even when obstacles or other people stand in the way.

Listen for Feelings, Not to Fix

When it comes to raising our little girls, the last thing we want is to see them in pain or facing adversity. Men, in general, are protectors, especially when it comes to our families. Perhaps that protector mentality is amplified even more when it comes to protecting our little girls. We protect from predators, danger, threats, pain, and even stress. Protecting is hard wired in our DNA as men. Ask any man, and we will tell you that we will step in front of a moving train at top speed to rescue anyone in our family and especially our little girls. Men will get between their daughters and anything that will threaten them physically, mentally, emotionally, and spiritually.

Believe it or not, this important and critical part of us as men can be a disservice to raising our daughters, meaning we can use this critical skill of protection or fixing at the wrong times. The most common time we see this used improperly is when our daughters come to us with a problem. The problem can be a variety of different things. Problems can show up as: being bullied in school, issues with her self-image, performance in school, performance in sports, problems with boys, issues and drama with friends, etc. The list of problems and challenges that arise with our girls (boys too) can be endless.

The good news is that we, as men, embrace it when problems arise. We find a lot of joy, satisfaction, and validation knowing that we helped solve a problem or relieved some pain. However, most of the time, this isn't what our daughters want or need. Our daughters have the same needs as our wives. They need to feel seen, heard, safe, and validated. As we covered in the Husband section of this book, our wives don't always want us to fix it. In fact, *most* of the time, they don't want us to fix the problem or rescue them. What they truly want is to be seen, heard, safe, and validated. Again, this isn't all the time. At times, your wife absolutely wants some help with solving a problem or even making a big decision. What I have seen work the best is using the "80/20 rule." Eighty percent of the time, she wants you to listen and be empathetic. She is seeking validation and connection, not the rescue. Twenty percent of the time, she is looking for you to lead or collaborate on a solution. Our daughters are no different.

If you really want to shoot straight for her heart when she is dealing with adversity, problems, or overwhelm, simply listen. She needs you to hear her because she wants to connect with you. She wants to be seen because she wants to feel safe with you. She wants her feelings validated by her dad because Dad's validation of what she is feeling hits her right in the heart.

When she comes to you with any type of struggle, don't just listen for the words; listen and be in tune with the emotions she might be feeling. Don't get distracted analyzing and brainstorming solutions to her problems. Simply listen for feelings, identify what you think she is feeling, and validate those emotions. Believe it or not, when it comes to being the protector of our daughters, a big part of that is helping her feel safe. Protection is all about safety, and when it comes to emotions, listening and helping her identify what she is feeling goes much further than diving right in and giving advice. Don't get me wrong; this isn't all the time. There are times she will come to you because she wants help solving something she is facing, and she is looking to her dad to be that man too. It can be confusing, and at times, we have no clue which one she wants. So, if you don't know, ask.

One of my favorite ways to ask my wife if she needs help solving a problem or if she just wants me to listen is: "Sweetheart, sounds like you are facing something big. Would you like me to just listen, or do you want me to help with some advice? I'm good either way. Which one feels right to you?"

I've seen this question work extremely well. It's almost always received well because when you ask a question like this, it shows you had the emotional IQ to check in with her on which one would be most meaningful. When it comes to our daughters (and wives), I'm also a big fan of using "feeling words" instead of "thinking words." Notice in the example above I used, "Which one **FEELS** right?" I didn't ask, "Which one do you think you need?" I do that purposefully and with intention because our daughters (especially when in a heightened emotional state) are more focused on what they are feeling about the situation. When we use more feeling words, it shows we are more in tune and connected with them on an emotional level.

When it comes to listening, listen for what she is feeling, notice her body language, be aware of her voice tone, and label the emotions she might be feeling. The more you help her identify what she might be feeling, the better listener you become.

Once we have identified what she is feeling, it's important to validate her feelings by being empathetic. Don't be sympathetic; be empathetic. There's huge difference. Dr. Brene Brown describes empathy as a skill that can bring people together and make people feel included, while sympathy creates an uneven power dynamic and can lead to more isolation and disconnection. After you have validated and reflected back, it's time to invite her to tell you more. Stay away from using the word "why." Remember, the word "why" will put people on the defense and even make them feel condescended.

After you have labeled her emotional state and validated her, invite her to tell you more; allow her to say anything else that is on her mind and in her heart. I'm a huge fan of inviting her to tell you more because you will most likely get more information that you otherwise wouldn't, but she will get even more clarity as she talks through the issue on a deeper level.

Once you have finished all of the above and she has gotten everything out, it's time for the final question. This final question is extremely powerful for both her and you for many reasons. Before I get to the reasons, let me share the question. The question is this: "Sweetheart, this situation sounds so overwhelming. Who wouldn't be overwhelmed by what you are facing? I feel so honored you shared everything you did with me. How can I best support you? What feels right?"

That last question is a gamechanger for you and her. When you validate her feelings, normalize her feelings, and praise her for coming to you, this final question shows that you are there to provide any support that she identifies that she needs from you. You also used "What **FEELS** right?" not "What can I do for you?" The interesting thing about ending with this question is that she will most likely be clear on what support she needs from you. She might say that she just needed you to listen and be there, which is awesome! She might tell you that she just needed to vent so she could get more clarity on the situation, which is awesome! She also might ask you to help her find a solution or ask for your advice, which is awesome!

At the end of a conversation like this, she will view you as her knight in shining armor. She will feel seen, heard, safe, and validated, which is exactly what she needs from you. To add in a little bonus here, since she experienced all of that with you, the likelihood of her coming to you again with something she needs help with is extremely high.

Just to put a bow on all of this:

1. When she comes to you with a problem, issue, or something overwhelming, listen to her words, be aware of her emotions and identify them, and validate. When you do this for her, she feels seen, heard, safe, and validated. For you, this will make you a much better listener and in tune with her on a higher level.

2. Listen to validate and not always to fix. When we listen to validate and not fix, she will feel more seen, heard, and safe with you. When you are not focused on fixing, you are 100 percent in the moment, listening. Your mind isn't wandering into solution mode.

3. If you don't know if you should listen or advise, just ask. Remember to use questions like, "What **FEELS** right?" She is in a heightened emotional state, so using "feeling words" will hit her more in the heart. And don't worry; after asking, she will usually tell you. At that point, you now know where the conversation is going and what your role is.

4. Towards the end of the conversation, validate her again and ask the question, "How can I best support you? What **FEELS** right?" She will love this because this truly makes her feel safe. She will also tell you what support she needs, and then it will be clear to you what you need to do.

5. Finally, praise her for coming and talking to you. Let her know that you enjoyed the conversation. Let her know you recognize that it took courage to come and talk to you about something that was difficult. Encourage her to keep coming to you.

You Are Already Her HERO

Many of us are very familiar with Dr. Meg Meeker. She is a popular speaker and has written several bestselling books on the topic of parenthood, such as the national bestseller, *Hero: Being the Strong Father Your Kids Need*, *The 10 Habits of Happy Mothers*, *Boys Should be Boys,* and the most popular, *Strong Father, Strong Daughters*.

Dr. Meeker has spent more than 30 years practicing pediatric and adolescent medicine and counseling teens and parents. She is a fellow of the National Advisory Board of the Medical Institute and an associate professor of medicine at Michigan State School of Human Medicine.

Over the past several years, I have gotten to know Dr. Meg and her work extremely well. Not only have I read all of her books, but I have also had her on the podcast twice, and she was a keynote speaker at our annual event, The Dad Edge Summit, in 2021.

Dr. Meg is powerful voice in the fatherhood space, and for good reason. When I first came across Dr. Meg's work, I wondered what a woman, mom, and pediatrician knew about fatherhood. If I am being totally honest, I was a bit taken aback because she isn't a dad. *What could she possibly know about these topics?* I wondered. After getting to know Dr. Meg for the past several years, I have learned that she is extremely open and owns the fact that she doesn't know fatherhood firsthand, but what she does know are kids! Over the past 30 years, she has heard the stories, the wounds, the victories, and the hardships of children as it relates to their relationship with their dads. She writes her books on parenthood, and fatherhood, from the perspective of the impacts she has seen in kids, families, and even moms/dads individually. She helps her readers get a view and perspective from our kids' vantage point. In other words, she helps us to see ourselves as dads through the eyes of our kids. When we really dive into her work, it's extremely powerful.

As men raising daughters, we usually view our parenting perspective through our own lens, and to be honest, we are extremely critical of ourselves. We can actually be so critical and cruel when it comes to our shortcomings that it causes a lot of us to disengage from being the best version of ourselves with our daughters.

Dr. Meg reminds us that we are already our daughters' heroes. She goes on to state that we are the first men in our daughters' lives. For a woman's entire life, half of her heart belongs to her dad. She already views you as her hero, and for the most part, we (as dads) don't see that. We are too busy pointing out all of our flaws and shortcomings. We are too busy critiquing all the things we are doing wrong and how we miss the mark.

Dr. Meg encourages us to look at ourselves through the lens of our daughters. She loves you. She believes in you. You are her world. You are her provider and protector. You are strong but also gentle. You are the one who checks the closets and under the bed to protect her from the monsters. You are the one who she views as her foundation when she starts dating and even when she gets her heart broken. You are the one that she will turn if she is getting bullied at school. When she scores the goal in her game, she will look to see you in the crowd. You are the hero in her life. Accept it. Embrace it and act the part.

She will measure every man that comes in her life up against you. Remember, regardless of the men that come in and out of her life, you are the first. At the end of the day, she seeks validation from you when it comes to any man who comes into her world. She is watching your every move as it relates to how you love her mom. She is learning from her hero what true male love, affection, and safety is all about. She already believes in you, and all we need to do is act the part.

Now, you might be reading this book when your daughter is in her teen years. Perhaps you are experiencing the opposite of what I am talking about here. In other words, you feel that your relationship with your daughter is strained or distant. Perhaps you feel that your daughter doesn't even like you. You might feel that she looks at you like you are the villain and not the hero. You might even feel this when you try to give your daughter a hug and she doesn't really hug you back. Perhaps she goes to her mom for everything she needs and basically neglects you completely. This can be an extremely confusing time for us dads. We feel like we are missing the mark big time with her. We might even feel regret that we didn't take more opportunities when she was younger to connect with her or maybe we did something wrong when she was younger altogether. We can feel hurt, angry, and even resentful if or when our daughters hit this stage. It's at this critical time when our daughters need us to double down on being the hero in their lives regardless of how they are acting towards us.

Dr. Meg talks a lot about this season of life with dads and daughters as well. The teenage time for girls and the relationship with their dad can feel tricky or even like a field of land mines with very little enjoyment. Some of us might wonder, *What happened to my little girl?* Dr. Meg shares so many examples of how normal these feelings can be during these years and how important it is that we stay the course of continuing to show up, engage, and be intentional with her. Her message is loud, clear, and makes total sense. The message is this: keep being the hero regardless of the outcome. If you hug her and she doesn't seem interested, oh well. Hug her every single day anyway. If you try to strike up conversation and she doesn't seem like she wants to talk, be interested and engage anyway. If it seems like she goes to her mom for every single thing she needs, don't lose hope. Continue to show up. When our daughters are younger, the hero role can feel easier because to her, you are larger than life. When she gets into the teenage years, it can feel much harder. However, it's actually more important and impactful that you double down on these efforts despite the outcomes because it will set the tone for your relationship with her when she is older.

As your daughter gets older, she will appreciate the effort and the fact you never faltered on your mission to be her hero, protector, and provider. She will look back on those years and appreciate the resilience you displayed. She will always appreciate the fact you never stopped trying. She will respect you because you stayed within your integrity despite her being distant during these years. It will also teach her the lifelong lesson of never giving up on your kids no matter what. She will remember you as the knight in shing armor who remained her hero despite how challenging it might have been. On the flip side, she will absolutely remember her dad giving up on her and disengaging because he wasn't getting what he needed back if you take the other path. If we really peel back the onion layer on this topic, if we disengage, get resentful, and step out of this power, we are teaching her to do the same in her relationships with her kids. By now, you are most likely recognizing that this work doesn't start and stop with you. Your role as a husband and father is legacy and generational work. The foundation you create today will trickle down to your kids and even your grandchildren.

The lesson is this: you are already her hero whether she views you as such right now or 40 years from now. Heroes don't give up and they don't falter. Heroes run into burning buildings while everyone else is running out because they are focused on stepping up. Heroes operate with integrity and humility, and they stay the course without being tied to outcome. Be her hero when it's easy and be her hero when it's hard. I promise it will make all the difference.

Your Words Will Create Her World

Most of us remember the tone of voice and the words our fathers used when speaking to us. Some of the words used created wounds so deep that they are difficult for us to talk about or even look back on. Other words our fathers might have used when speaking to us inspired us to be able to do anything with our lives. The words of a father remain in his children's hearts forever and become their inner voice and compass when they get older.

I would argue that when it comes to the words and messages we use, it is even more impactful to our daughters because the dynamic between dad and daughter is different. It's not better or worse than the relationship between a dad and son; it's just different. In general, our daughters seek our hearts. At the end of the day, daughters desperately want and need to be at their dads' heart centers. As our daughters get older, that doesn't change. During their teenage years, as our daughters grow into young women, we might experience some distancing or even tension with them, but that need to be at the center of their dad's heart is still there. It doesn't go away...ever. Our daughters view our words as truth.

Going back to an interview I had with Dr. Meg Meeker, she really hit this point home that daughters take their dads' words as gold. Dr. Meg shared a story about her own father growing up that she has not only written about in her books, but she has seen the exact same theme emerge in several other daughters over the years.

After Dr. Meg graduated with her bachelor's degree, she applied to several medical schools in hopes of becoming a pediatrician. Her father was a physician, and she saw how much he loved it. She was inspired to go to medical school and follow in his footsteps. She didn't have a "Plan B." Being a pediatrician was it! After applying to several medical schools and getting rejection letter after rejection letter, she became frustrated and felt defeated. At 21 years old, she was forced to move back home. She thought that her dream of becoming a doctor was over and now, at 21 years old, she would have to find something else to do. The problem was she didn't want to do anything else. To add insult to injury, she felt so devastated that she had to resort to being supported by her parents and moving back home. She felt that she had not only let herself down, but her dad as well. After all, her dad was a successful physician and had been in practice for decades. It was interesting to hear her perspective as I interviewed her because we can all relate to not only failure but to feeling like we have failed our dads.

The truth of the matter was her dad never stopped believing in her. He never scolded her for not getting into medical school. He never said he was disappointed in her. Instead, he poured words of encouragement into her. However, one of the most powerful ways he poured words of encouragement into her was what he said when he didn't think she was listening.

Dr. Meg recalls a time just after she moved back home when she heard her dad on a phone call with a colleague. She didn't pay much attention to the conversation at first, but her ears perked up when she realized that he was talking about her.

The colleague asked how Meg was doing. Her dad replied, "She is doing great. We are happy to have her home, but she won't be here long because she will be going to medical school within the next 12 months."

Hearing her dad say this about her hit her in such a profound way. She started wondering, *What does he know that I don't? Why would he say that? After all, I have been rejected by so many schools! Did he pay someone off to get me into school, or did he hear from a school that I didn't?*

Meg went on to share that, of course, her dad would never pay any school off. In fact, he wasn't the type of man to even get on the phone with a school to try and pull some strings. The answer from her father to the colleague came from one place...from his heart. He believed with every part of his being that despite being rejected by several medical schools, she was destined to fulfill her dream no matter what. He believed in her and he said it out loud with his words. Taking this to the next level, he didn't just say it to her; he said it to others.

Dr. Meg took his words to heart, and something in her mind completely shifted. She knew in that moment that she no longer needed a "Plan B." Come hell or high water, she was going to medical school and she was going to become a pediatrician. Those words from her dad created her new world of possibilities. Can you imagine for a moment if her dad did nothing but share how disappointed he was in her or how much she let him down? If he would have brought blame, shame, and pain to her at this point in her life, most likely Dr. Meg wouldn't have gone to medical school, and the world wouldn't have her bestselling books. Believe it or not, the world as we know it would be missing something that she has brought to so many. Her books alone have over 10,000 five-star reviews on just Amazon alone. Keep in mind that most people who buy books never leave a review. She has impacted so many fathers over the years and by doing so, she has impacted our kids. This is such a powerful reminder to us as we raise our daughters that our words are critical. Our words can help her create new possibilities or destroy them.

Raising a daughter can be difficult and challenging at times. We are trying to do so much and we can get overwhelmed in the things that really don't matter. When it comes to the voice and the words we use when speaking to our daughters or about them, we have the ability to be their launching pads in life.

PART 4
LEADER

21 LEAD YOURSELF FIRST!

> *"True leadership mastery begins when you F.L.Y. – First Lead Yourself!"*
> — Elizabeth McCormick

When we think of leadership, many of us think of great leaders. We think of Leonidas leading the mighty 300 Spartans in the Battle of Thermopylae. We think of great presidents like Abraham Lincoln who changed history for the United States. We might even think of the best leader of all, Jesus Christ, and how he lived.

When we think of leading, we usually think about leading and inspiring others first. Great leadership actually doesn't start with leading others; it starts with leading ourselves. We can't possibly lead others effectively unless we can first lead ourselves.

When we start our adult lives and our careers, get married, and start having kids, as men we focus on leading and serving others while completely putting ourselves on the backburner. This feels noble, but it results in catastrophic outcomes. In order to effectively lead in our careers, we must learn to lead ourselves. In order to effectively lead in our marriages, we must learn to lead ourselves. In order to effectively lead our kids, we must learn to lead ourselves.

If you look at leaders above, they not only led others, but they led themselves extremely well. They didn't just do the work to be a great leader; they were the work. It was part of their being and who they were.

Leonidas not only expected his warriors to go through the Agoge; he had to do it himself successfully. He didn't just expect his warriors to fight for Sparta; he was the first one on the front lines, ready to fight with them. He didn't just expect his soldiers to be in top fighting shape; he was expected to be in fighting shape himself. Because he effectively led himself and he learned the skills of resilience, mental toughness, physical readiness, and love of his country, he was also able to lead his soldiers to do the same.

Jesus Christ didn't just preach the Word of God; he lived it. He was the shining example of living a sinless life in accordance with God's Word. He didn't just tell his apostles how to live and preach the Word of God; he was the example by his actions and living his purpose. He led himself effectively and by doing so, he led others extremely well.

Leading Ourselves by Building Trust First

When we think of leadership, we automatically think of leading, inspiring, and influencing others. We think about great leaders that we admire from history that are well known or even great leaders that we have had in our lives. While its always amazing to lead others, we often overlook one of the most critically important attributes of leading others. We must first gain their trust. People (including our kids) will not follow us or will be reluctant to follow us if they don't trust us. Keep in mind that trust is earned, not given. There is a price to pay for trust, and the rent is paid every day by earning it.

22 RULES FOR LEADERSHIP

> *"A father is neither an anchor to hold us back nor a sail to take us there, but a guiding light whose love shows us the way."*
> — Unknown

Rule #1: Be a Man of Your Word

Bottom line, if you say you are going to do something, do it. PERIOD. If you promise your son or daughter you will play catch when you get home from work, do it. If you say you will help with homework, do it. If you promise your daughter that you will play dress up and attend the tea party with her dolls, do it. If you promise your wife that you will complete that project by this weekend, do it. Your kids are always watching your every move, and we are leading by example. If trust is broken, and we aren't men of our word, we can never expect our kids to look to us as a trusted leader.

Rule #2: Be the Lighthouse, Not the Tugboat in the Storm

Another powerful way to earn trust is to be the calm in the storm of chaos. When we have kids, life can be really unpredictable. Chaos is always around the corner. Kids will do things wrong. Things will be broken. There will be fighting among siblings. There will be heated moments and wrongdoings. There will be meltdowns and tantrums. A trusted leader remains calm and doesn't give into emotional moments when everything is falling apart. Two examples I love that truly hit this point home are the calm ship captain and the lighthouse in the storm.

Imagine you are on a ship at sea. Suddenly, the ship stops moving and the engine dies. You and everyone aboard are in the middle of nowhere without another ship in sight for rescue. How would you feel about your captain if he suddenly freaked out and started to panic, not knowing what to do or how to respond? Chances are you would panic and become worried you wouldn't make it out of the situation alive. On the other hand, think about how you would feel if the captain remained calm, got on the intercom, and let everyone know not to worry. This captain tells you the ship is having engine issues, but he has called for help, and a rescue ship is 15 miles away and in route. How would that make you feel? Confident? Calm? The captain is calm, and he knows what to do, which makes the passengers and crew confident. Passengers and crew members are calm because they trust the leadership of the captain.

Now imagine a lighthouse in a vicious storm. No matter how bad the storm is or how hard the wind blows, the lighthouse remains steady and lights the way for the boats coming into shore. The lighthouse does its job of staying strong and steady for the boats to make their way back to shore. It doesn't get involved with the intensity of the storm nor does it get into the ferocious waters with the boats. It simply lights the way for the boats to come to shore. The captains of those boats trust the steady guiding light from the lighthouse. The light from the lighthouse is always consistent and never changing, and that's why it is trusted.

The same goes for us. Kids are always watching our every move, especially in the heat of chaos. If we panic, so will they. If we give into the chaos, so will they. Trusted leaders remain calm in the storm. That is why they are trusted.

Rule #3: Be the Safe Place for Them to Land When Things Go Badly in Their Lives

Being a father means we have a lot of skin the game relative to things that go on in our kids' lives, how they respond, and mistakes they make. If you were anything like me when you were growing up, you were terrified to make a mistake or screw up in front of your parents. Usually, when mistakes were addressed in my house, they were accompanied by guilt, shame, and blame. As a result, I was fearful to screw up in any way because it meant I was going to experience a barrage of guilt and shame.

Kids are going to mess up and make mistakes as they grow up. They will be dishonest from time to time. They will get caught doing something wrong. If there is a great deal of trust, they will come to you and tell you before you have a chance to find out on your own. When mistakes are made or if our kids come to us during a low point, it's our job to be a safe place for them to land. It's important for us to respond with calm and safety. Now, let's get one thing straight for those of you who are thinking this means there is an absence of discipline. Safety is not the absence of consequences. Safety is how we respond with our voice and words. There can and still will be consequences for wrongdoings, but we can do it without the shame and guilt. Fair and just consequences are still important because they teach the lesson; however, responding with calm without the guilt and shame is critical.

Think of this in our professional lives. When we screw up in the workplace, how does our boss respond? Do they respond with calm, or do they respond with guilt, shame, and blame? Think of the last time you made a mistake at work. How did your boss handle it, AND how did you respond to how your boss handled it? Perhaps your boss responded with calm and simply helped you solve the issue. You most likely walked away from that experience feeling pretty damn good about not only the situation but the relationship you have with your boss. The level of trust most likely increased, and it only made you want to work harder for him or her. On the flip side, if there was yelling, guilt, shame, blame, and he/she scolded you, you most likely walked away from that situation feeling ten times worse. Most likely you felt so horrible, you went and updated your resume and jumped on LinkedIn. You also made a mental note to never go to him/her with a mistake again because you feared the ramifications. The trust was broken, and your boss (and perhaps even your job) was no longer safe. People will follow a leader who can respond to chaos with calm. Be the calm in the storm. Be the lighthouse for the boats. Be the captain of your ship.

Rule #4: Great Leaders Use High-Quality Questions to Teach Lessons, Not Lectures

If your upbringing was anything like mine, it was filled with lectures. Our parents were experts at lecturing us growing up. Lectures are neither right nor wrong; they just aren't as effective as high-quality questions to get the other person thinking.

When we are guiding and leading our kids, usually our default strategy is to share all of our words of wisdom and knowledge by using a lot of words. We want to give our kids every bit of knowledge we can possibly muster on any given topic where we have experience. Truth of the matter, our kids will tune us out after so much time. We will begin to sound like the teacher from Charlie Brown. If you don't believe me, just watch your kids' eyes glaze over as you continue to pour your life experience and wisdom into them. I am not saying that your intentions aren't good, but I am saying there is a more effective way. Great leaders don't lecture. Great leaders ask high-quality questions to engage the people they are leading so they can help them with the solution. Not only do great leaders ask high-quality questions, but they also believe that their wisdom may or may not be the best. A lot of times, the people we are leading have the best solutions to issues. When it comes us leading our kids, asking high-quality questions instead of lecturing them will be more effective in a lot of cases.

As I write this book, my two oldest boys are 16 and 14. These are the prime ages for peer pressure for all kinds of crazy things these kids have access to. I have had several conversations (not lectures) about the dangers of drugs and alcohol. As the boys' father, guide, and leader, I used to be so tempted to simply lecture and share all my wisdom on the dangers of drugs and alcohol. A few times, when they were younger, I did get on my high horse and do more of a lecture and share of wisdom to explain why it was important that they don't give into peer pressure and start going down a path of substance abuse. I would always notice that glazed/glossed-over look in their eyes. I could tell they weren't listening. It was just another lecture.

Just a few months ago, one of them came to me to tell me that their circle of friends were getting into not only vaping but weed and alcohol. I didn't lecture, even though part of me badly wanted to. Instead, I started asking deeper questions to engage and lead them in the conversation.

Son: "Dad, a few of my friends are really getting into vaping, smoking weed, and even drinking."

Me: "Wow...thanks for telling me that. What do you think about all of that?"

Son: "Dad, I hate it."

Me: "You hate it? Tell me more."

Son: "I hate it because it's so bad for you. I am worried about them."

Me: "Tell me what you know about it and why you are worried."

Son: "Well, I know vaping is really bad for you because it's really bad for your lungs. I am an athlete and I never want anything to get in the way of performing on the field. I would be afraid that I would be winded and maybe not able to think as quickly if I was doing that stuff. I don't understand the alcohol thing. Alcohol smells terrible, and I am sure it tastes terrible. It's really bad for your health. It makes you put on weight and makes you slower. I wouldn't want that."

Me: "Wow, man...you are spot on with all of that! I'm guessing at this point, they have most likely asked you or maybe even pressured you to try it?"

Son: "Yes, many times. I have spoken up about how bad it is for them. I actually took my friend's vape and threw it in the woods. He got so pissed at me. But I am watching out for them, and they have no clue how bad it is for them. They got really mad at me, but I didn't care."

Me: "Wow, you are a true leader! It's awesome that you are sharing some of the negative effects of what they are doing. How might you lead them even more effectively when you are around them?"

Son: "I just need to be the example! I love playing football and I am viewed as a leader on my team and in my circle of friends. By me being the example and not giving in, maybe that will inspire them to stop or not do it as much. Maybe if I tell them about how I am able to run faster during practices or share how much my bench press has gone up, it will inspire them to stay healthier."

Me: "I think you are spot on with all of that! By being the example and leading the way, people will take notice. I really appreciate you telling me all of this and I think you have a really good head on your shoulders. You are right about health and performance. If you are doing that stuff, it will hinder your progress. So, nice job recognizing that."

The above conversation was an example of one of many conversations I have had with my two oldest boys. If you notice, when my son was responding to my questions, he was not only articulating what I would have lectured him on; he actually added more things I wouldn't even thought of. True leaders ask high-quality questions for the other side to lead themselves. There is a time and a place for lectures. For the most part, if you become a master in asking high-quality questions, you don't need to lecture. They will not only articulate the solution, but most likely add things you weren't thinking of.

Rule #5: When You Ask Your Kids to Do Something... EXPLAIN WHY

Back in 2018, I had the honor of interviewing one the most highly decorated Navy SEALs, Jocko Willink. Jocko Willink is a decorated, retired U.S. Navy Seal Officer, the author of several books, two of which include *Extreme Ownership* and *Dichotomy of Leadership*. He is the co-founder of Echelon Front, where he is a leadership instructor, speaker, and executive coach.

Jocko has spent 20 years in the U.S. Navy Seal Teams, starting as an enlisted SEAL and rising through the ranks to become a SEAL officer. As Commander of SEAL Team 3's Task Unit "Bruiser" during the Battle of Ramadi, he orchestrated SEAL operations that helped the ready-first brigade of the U.S. Army's first armored division to bring stability to the violent war-torn city. Task Unit "Bruiser" became the most highly decorated Special Operations unit of the Iraq War.

Jocko returned from Iraq to serve as an officer in charge of training for all West Coast SEAL Teams. There, he spearheaded the development of leadership training and personally instructed and mentored the next generation of SEAL leaders who have continued to perform with great success on the battlefield.

During his career, Jocko Willink was awarded the Silver Star, the Bronze Star, and numerous other personal and unit awards. In 2010, he retired from the Navy and launched Echelon Front with Leif Babin, where he teaches the leadership principles he learned on the battlefield to help others lead and win. Clients include individuals, teams, companies, and organizations across a wide range of industries and fields.

He shared several amazing tactics on not only leading people and teams but also raising our kids. One of the most important tactics he shared was always telling people, teams, and our KIDS why we are doing what we are doing or what they need to do.

When our kids ask "Why?" to a request from us, or if they just need to know why we are doing what we are doing, it can be tempting to respond with "Because I said so."

If you are anything like me, you were used to hearing that response growing up. Maybe you heard, "Because I am the parent and you are the kid…that's why! Now go do it!"

While that may feel right in the moment to say to our kids, it provides zero clarity or even skin in the game for them to execute what needs to be done.

One example Jocko shared was getting kids to clean their room. Most kids hate doing it, and they truly don't see the value in keeping their rooms clean. Jocko shared that one of the reasons why he expects his kids to keep their room kept is because in case of an emergency situation, the kids will be able to get what they need out of their rooms without tripping and falling over their clutter. We all know that could be a rare occurrence, but it's absolutely true. If there is an emergency and the family needs to evacuate the premises, a clean room, free of clutter on the floor, could be the difference between life and death during a fire or other emergency situation. Now, again, we all know that would be a rare occasion, but it is possible and an example of explaining WHY to our kids so they have clarity and know the importance of that task.

A personal example that I have shared with my boys is when they leave soaking wet towels or clothes are their carpeted floor for days at a time. In the past, I've been stern and have even yelled at them about this. For a long time, I never explained to them that the dangers could be mold that starts to grow within the carpeting on in their rooms and the health dangers that come with prolonged inhalation of mold.

Back in 2010, I was working in medical device sales. I had a buyer for a hospital who was not only a huge customer, but he was also a really good friend. He suddenly was hospitalized and became extremely ill for months. He couldn't return to work for nearly four months, and his illness seemed to come out of nowhere. Upon investigation of his symptoms, it was believed he was breathing toxic mold for quite a long time. His house was free and clear of mold upon inspection. However, it was found that the mold was coming from his office. Apparently, there had been a very slow leak (only small drops) coming in from his office window during rainstorms, and over time, the slow water leak went behind his wall and into the carpet under the window. Just a few drops here and there on a weekly basis turned into a huge deadly mold problem that nearly took his life and impacted his health for years to come. His road to recovery wasn't easy. I remember seeing him at a hockey game before he officially returned to work and I didn't even recognize him upon first glance because he had lost so much weight, looked so frail, and looked like he aged 15 years.

After multiple times of being stern, yelling, and even punishing my boys for not complying, I learned this tactic wasn't working. Me simply telling them to do a task and not explaining why gave them no clarity or even skin in the game to do it. After I interviewed Jocko, I sat my kids down and told them the story about my customer and good friend. I shared with them the dangers of mold growth and how it impacts their health. I went on to explain how it would impact their sports performance and other aspects of their healthy lives. You could just see the light bulbs turning on. From that moment on, I never had to remind, yell, or punish. They simply kept wet clothes and towels off their floors in their rooms. Wet clothes and towels were hung up to dry.

One final point that will really hit this home. Think about your job or place of work. You play an important role at your company or within your business. There is a WHY behind everything that you do or what you are requested to do to move the business forward. Let's say your boss asked you to do something, and you weren't clear on the task or project, so you asked, "Why do I need to do (fill in the blank)?" If he or she responded with a condescending "BECAUSE I SAID SO! I'm the boss—that's why! Now go do it!", you would do it, but you would also be looking for another job.

Our kids are no different. We can motivate and lead by fear, but that doesn't deepen the respect or credibility we have with our kids. Plus, what lessons are we teaching them about authority and leadership if we do it poorly ourselves?

Rule #6: Never Stop Learning and Learn with Your Kids

The most successful people and leaders in the world are lifelong learners. The best leaders on the planet don't claim to have all the answers. However, they are open to learning the answers. Leaders constantly learn new skills. Not only do they learn new skills, but they surround themselves with people who have skills they haven't learned. The day we stop learning is the day we stop living and leading well.

When I was younger, I played some baseball, but I was terrible. I also played basketball, but I was terrible at that too. I wrestled in high school, and I was average at best. I wasn't the most athletic kid growing up. I was fat and out of shape. I actually didn't get fit until I was 17 years old. I always wanted to play football but didn't really understand the sport because I wasn't around it. After performing poorly in other sports, I had also concluded that I wasn't athletic enough to even try out. To be honest, that has been a huge regret for me. I have always wanted to learn how to play football but never got into it.

My 14 year old, Mason, started playing football when he was in third grade and fell in love with the sport. Up until he was in third grade, I coached Mason's baseball and wrestling teams. I was never the head coach of his team (never wanted to be), but I loved being one of the coaches. I knew how to play baseball and I knew wrestling. I loved teaching the kids skills and techniques in both sports. To be honest, I loved coaching, but I loved being with Mason more than anything.

When Mason wanted to start playing football at eight years old, I was really excited because I knew that I knew nothing about the sport and I was looking forward to just being a spectator. The first day of football practice, I showed up ready to watch Mason and be a part of his first day of football. I was standing off on the sidelines, just enjoying these little guys in their pads doing drills and learning the game.

I saw the head coach approaching me, and he extended his hand. He introduced himself and said, "Hey, I'm looking for one more coach to help out with the team, and you look like you probably played the game."

I smiled from ear to ear and laughed. I said, "I actually have never played. I know the bare basics of the game if that. I watch football and the Super Bowl, but that is about it."

He smiled back. "I just need another coach to help, hold the pads from time to time, and help me coordinate. You up for that?"

I smiled and said, "Why not? I'm in! Great opportunity to learn the game."

As the season went on, I literally became the running joke of not only the other coaches but the players too. It truly came out that I knew nothing about the game because I was always asking for clarity on what the positions were, what the plays meant, and even some of the lingo. Mid-season the coach came up to me, laughing, and said, "You weren't kidding! You know nothing about this game!" I became the running joke, but I didn't mind it because it added so much lightheartedness to the team. Even the boys would laugh at my expense.

About halfway through the season, Mason and I grabbed some Jimmy John's one night after practice. We were enjoying our food when he said, "Dad, can I ask you something?"

"Of course! Anything!" I said.

"Dad, I see the other coaches always making fun of you because you don't know the game. Even some of the players think it's funny that Coach Hagner doesn't know the game. Do you really not understand the game or even know what you are doing?" he asked with a smile.

I smiled ear to ear and asked, "You want to know a secret?"

He leaned in and whispered, "Yeah…"

I whispered back, "Mason, I have no clue what I am doing out there."

We both laughed. With a huge grin on his face and laughing he asked, "Why are you coaching then, Dad?"

I smiled back and said, "Mason, I've always wanted to learn the game of football. In fact, I have regretted never trying it growing up. When your coach asked me if I wanted to help, I thought it was not only a great opportunity to learn but an amazing opportunity to hang out with YOU! To me this is a huge win! I get to learn something and I get to be with my son. I could care less if the coaches and players laugh. In fact, I love it because it adds some fun and humor to the environment. I'm never too old or too good to learn something new. Plus, if I get to learn it with my kids, I will do that all day long! It's a great lesson for you too. Never ever stop learning! Never be afraid to learn something new. Learning new things isn't always easy, but it keeps us sharp!"

He smiled from ear to ear and said, "That's cool, Dad. I'm glad you are out there! It's fun."

I went on to help coach the team for the next two years after that. I was constantly learning new things. I loved it.

Mason has been playing football ever since that year for the past five seasons. We are often outside throwing the ball. He has been able to throw a perfect spiral for a long time. Throwing a spiral was something I have never been able to do. This past year, Mason took me under his wing and within 15 minutes, he showed me how to grip the ball and throw a perfect spiral. That is usually a skill we learn from our own dads or our coaches growing up. Not me. My 14-year-old son taught his old man how to do it. He loved the fact that he got to teach me that skill, and I loved the fact I learned from him.

Never stop learning, and let your kids see you learn. Not only that; if you really want to empower your kids, have them teach you something. It's an amazing experience and teaches them that LEADERS LEARN!

Rule #7: Push Your Kids Outside Their Comfort Zones WITHOUT Completely Overwhelming Them

Jocko Willink isn't the only Navy SEAL or Special Forces Operator I have had on the podcast. I have had the distinct honor of interviewing over 50 men who have served as SEALS, Rangers, Special Forces, etc. Several of them have shared absolute gold when it comes to this rule. Many of us don't push our kids hard enough or we go to the extreme of pushing our kids so hard that they crumble. The most effective thing we can do is to find the balance of the capabilities of our kids, pushing them out of their comfort zone just enough without completely overwhelming them to the point they crumble.

Building confidence in our kids doesn't happen overnight. It doesn't happen with one conversation or even one situation. It is built up over time and through elevating their perceived limitations.

In order to help our kids build confidence in themselves or something they are going to do, usually we have to take baby steps to push them gently out of their comfort zones. We can actually make the journey enjoyable if we know how to do it.

I will never forget a time years ago when I was at a public pool when my boys were little. There was a dad with a little boy who was around the age of six or seven. The little boy wanted to learn how to dive but was terrified to try it on his own. As my boys and I sat on the sidelines watching, we saw this dad crush his son. The dad demanded that his son climb up the diving board and dive right into the pool. Most likely for me or you, this wouldn't be a big deal. But for a six-year-old boy who has never done it, it was terrifying. The boy was crying and stood at the base of the ladder, screaming that he was scared. The more the boy cried, the louder his dad yelled. The dad was saying things like, "STOP CRYING! IT'S NOT THAT SCARY! BE A MAN! IT'S NO BIG DEAL! IT'S WATER! IT WON'T KILL YOU!" Maybe all that is true to some degree, but to this kid, this was a huge risk and something he had obviously never done. The situation ended after several minutes of this poor kid crying and his dad only yelling louder. The dad finally caved and gave up. Everyone who was watching could tell this situation was traumatic for the little boy and disappointing for the father. It wasn't easy to watch.

We all want our kids to be brave and take risks. We all want our kids to be "that kid" who can go out and do something that other kids fear. Some kids are braver than others, and some are more confident than others. The most important thing is we have to meet our kids where they are at and create steppingstones of wins with them.

My oldest was no different than this little boy growing up. He was terrified of the water when he was younger. I remember we would go to the pool, and for two summers he wouldn't go past the stairs going into the water. For the first season, he would sit on the side of the pool with his feet in and was absolutely terrified to go in. The following year, he would sit on the stairs in the pool but refused to go in past the stairs or the water past his chest. The more we pushed him, the more he would refuse. Jumping off of a diving board for him was completely out of the question. It took years, but we leveled up his confidence, but this required creating small wins and meeting him where he was at. For the first season, we encouraged him to move from the side of the pool where he dipped his feet in to sitting on the stairs where the water came to his chest. That's as far as he went for that whole season. The next year, we held him in the water with us. He was terrified, but we showed him he was safe with us, and we were also teaching him how to swim along the way. There were many days when he was scared, but it wasn't to the point where he was so overwhelmed. Eventually, he got more comfortable with swimming with us and us holding him. Then, we would move five feel away from him, and he would swim to us. Then, we would move 10 feet away. Then, we would move 15 feet away. Each milestone was celebrated, and you could see the confidence growing with each evolution. The following year, he wanted to learn how to jump in the water from the side of the pool. We tried to start him just jumping right in, but that was too much for him. We met him where he was at and had him jump to us so we could catch him. When he got that, we moved further and further away. After he got that, we then moved far enough away where he was just jumping in on his own without us catching him, but we were there in the water if he needed us. When he mastered that, he wanted to try the diving board. Of course, he was terrified at first, but he did it! He had tallied up enough wins and confidence to eventually go from only putting his feet in the water from the side of the pool to jumping off the diving board. Each evolution and milestone pushed him just further and just enough out of his comfort zone to where he felt fear but it wasn't paralyzing to him. It didn't overwhelm him to the point where he caved. He is now 16 years old and is one of our biggest risk takers. He loves challenges and takes them head on, in stages if he needs to.

A big part of leading our kids and helping them build confidence is meeting them where they are at and pushing them slightly out of their perceived comfort zones where they have a safe place to fail. Many of us want to take our kids from zero to 60 when it comes to situations, challenges, or milestones. The bottom line is this: know your kid, their abilities, and their perceived limitations. Our job isn't the beat them into submission to do something they otherwise wouldn't. That isn't fun for you or them. If you want to make the journey fulfilling for you and successful for them, meet them where they are at and push them SLIGHTLY, in steps, outside of their comfort zones.

Rule #8: Lead with Core Values

Leading with your core values is something that is foundational and critical to you as a man, father, husband, leader, and even human being. The words "core values" get kicked around a lot, but many of us don't really understand what they are, what our personal core values are, or how to lead with core values.

Every human being on the planet has core values. Some of us know what our core values are, and some of us have no clue what our core values are. Whether you consciously know what your values are or not, they are there within you.

Core values usually lie within our intuitional intelligence. We don't necessarily know what they are; we just know that we "feel something right or wrong" with regards to decisions we make or how we are operating.

Our underlying core values also show up in our business/or place of employment, our relationships, our parenting, and marriages. Again, for those of us who haven't gone through some sort of exercise to realize at a conscious level what our core values are, we usually don't exactly know what they are.

If you are scratching your head and wondering what your core values might be and how to even recognize them, not to worry; most people don't. Most people "feel" them but don't think about them.

If you have ever said, "I don't know what it is about (person/situation/thing), but it feels right to me." Or maybe you have said, "I don't know what it is about (person/situation/thing), but my gut is telling me this isn't good." That, my friend, is one of your core values trying to get your attention. When we think with our gut, or respond with our intuition, these are our core values speaking to us.

Let's take it a step further. I have no doubt that you have dated a woman in the past (or most likely it's the woman you are married to now), and you have said, "I don't know what it is about this woman, but it feels RIGHT! Everything about being with her seems right and easy. We get along so well, and it seems effortless. We have so much in common." Chances are your core values and hers are in alignment.

On the flip side, we have all dated women and said, "I don't know it is about this her, but it doesn't feel right to me. Something seems off, but I can't figure out why. My gut tells me she is not the one." Chances are your core values weren't in alignment with each other.

The same is said for friends and even the company we work for. I've known so many men who have high-paying jobs and titles behind their names, but they are absolutely miserable. When being asked why they are miserable, they usually respond with, "I don't really know. Something about this job doesn't feel good. I make great money and I able to provide anything for my family, but something about it doesn't seem right." When I hear this, I know that this man's core values and the values of the position or company are not in alignment. When people feel alive within their place of work, it's always because that company or position is in alignment with their deepest core values. Again, most people can't quite put their finger on it; they only know it feels really right or really wrong.

There are 150 human core values, and every human being operates within five to seven primary core values. Ninety-nine percent of the human race will go to their grave never bringing their deepest core values from the subconscious to the conscious level. We just go through life operating or even making decisions that we think might be right for us, but we really aren't sure. Add this to the skill set of being an effective leader, and defining our core values will make or break us and the people we are leading.

My core values are:

1. Family: The entire foundation of my business is helping families thrive. By doing so, I constantly get to learn how I can thrive with my family.

2. Connection: I am ultimately connected to my purpose in my life. I also know how to connect with my wife, kids, and community.

3. Community: Most men live a quiet life of isolation. We are physically surrounded by people constantly. As we age and take more in life, we tend to mentally and emotionally drift from others. My position with Dad Edge provides me with constant interaction with other dads and families.

4. Vitality: My physical, mental, and emotional health are top priorities for me. I have built a business around my life and not the other way around. Because I have done that, I am able to schedule time for physical exercise on a daily basis. Because I take time for self-care, my mental and emotional health are in alignment.

5. Adventure: I love taking adventures and seeing new places with my family. When I jump on a plane, I usually have one of my boys with me, my wife, or the whole family in tow, and when I travel for speaking events, I simply ask the host to pay for my family to fly and our lodging in exchange for a lower speaker fee.

6. Freedom: Because of my business, I govern my work time and my freedom. I do not work on someone else's timecard.

7. Faith: My faith has always been a part of my life; however, in the past three years it has become foundational. I truly believe that I am doing the work that God has put me on this earth to do. I take time every morning for prayer. Our family attends church every week. My faith is directly tied to my work, my family, and my spirit.

Before doing this work with men, husbands, and fathers, I was in the medical device sales industry for 17 years. I started in the industry in 2003 making an easy six figures. I stayed in a sales role for seven years until 2010. I loved the job and interacting with my customers. I didn't travel a whole lot. I had a local territory. I was home every night for dinner. I won sales awards every year. I was a performer and did well financially. I loved my role. Looking back, I thrived in that role because it allowed me to live within my core values as a husband, father, and human being. I had a deep, meaningful connection with my customers. I was home every night, which allowed me to have deep meaningful connection with my family. I love our home environment, and my job allowed me to be home every night. I didn't travel, and my job had balance, so I had time to take care of my health and vitality. The job was always an adventure. Every day was different because I was always in surgery with my surgeons. Every case was unique and different, which made the job adventurous. I had the community of an outstanding boss and my team, who I spoke with daily, and loved it. My boss and company always challenged me to grow my sales skills so I could achieve more aggressive quotas. My boss was an incredible mentor and family man. He had four boys as well. We had a solid relationship, and family was everything to us. Everything about the job felt right, and I thrived in every aspect of my life.

As with any sales role, when you do well, you are identified to move up the corporate ladder and go into management. In 2010, I was promoted to a regional manager position. I went from a small local territory where I was home every night to managing 12 states and 10 sales reps. On paper the job was great! I got a huge bump in salary. I got stock options with the company. A massive increase in my expense budget for travel, meals, my cell phone bill, my internet bill, and a seat at the table with the other big-wig executive management team. WOW! Life felt amazing! And then it didn't!

At first, I thought the job was glamorous. I was making a ton of money. I was able to provide an income I never thought possible.

We were even able to move from a small home to a bigger, nicer house. This also meant Jessica could continue to stay home with the boys without question. I started traveling three days a week. I had office days on Mondays and Fridays. I was gone working with my team Tuesday through Thursday (sometimes gone Monday through Friday). I was on planes and in rental cars and hotels every week. My airline status quickly rose, and I was racking up free flights faster than I could count. I achieved executive elite status with my favorite rental car company. I had reached platinum status with my favorite hotel chain within warp speed. Before I knew it, I had more free rentals with my rental car company, more free nights with my favorite hotel chain, and enough airline points to fly my family around the world.

I also started reporting to the VP of sales, who was an absolute toxic ball buster with zero work-life balance. I was one of five managers that worked for her. Her entire life was work, and she had zero connection in her marriage or with her two boys. Our management team would get emails at 2:00 a.m. and on weekends. Everything was business.

I was so busy with work and travel I wasn't making time to take care of my health. I was gaining weight eating on the road and sleeping in hotels. Within months, I was miserable, and I couldn't figure out why. All I knew is that I felt miserable in my gut. Something was telling me this didn't feel right, but I didn't know why. *Isn't this what I always wanted? I have more income than I ever dreamed I would have had. I have the nice house and nice car. I have the cool title after my name on my business cards and a seat at the table with the big wigs.* I got to the point where I hated packing my bag every week. I dreaded sleeping in another hotel or being in an airport. I couldn't stand the corporate bullshit and the political game of the corporate world. I got to thinking that there was something wrong with me! Everyone I knew would do anything to have this problem. It wasn't until I went through this core values exercise, and it hit me like a wrecking ball. It all made sense, and the pieces of the puzzle all came together.

The reason I wasn't happy is because that job was completely out of line with my core values. I was constantly away from my home *environment*. I loved being home and with my family. Other managers I worked with thrived being on the road and embraced getting away from their families. They loved it. I hated it. The *deep, meaningful connection* I had with my family plummeted because I was never around. My boys barely saw their dad. My wife and I were like ships passing in the night. She began to feel like a single mom. My health and *vitality* plunged because I was no longer taking care of my physical body, which also impacted my mental/emotional health. I didn't have the positive *community* or mentor in my life because my boss was such a ball buster who had zero work/life balance. You would think this might fulfill my sense of *adventure*, being able to travel so many places. Being in medical device sales meant traveling to a city but being stuck in a surgical OR for hours. Every OR looks the same; it didn't matter what city or place it was. There were times I would wake up in a hotel and couldn't remember what city I was in. On top of everything, because I was so miserable, I didn't have much of a sense of *humor*. Everything I was doing and how I was operating had nothing to do with more core values and what I valued most, but I didn't realize it at the time. I stuck with that career for several more years, thinking that life, fulfillment, and satisfaction would somehow improve. It never did until I understood what was truly important to me.

Once I realized my core values, I was able to understand why some of my relationships worked and some didn't. I also understood why understood why some parts of my home life were working and why some weren't. I also understood why I was physically, mentally, emotionally, and spiritually healthier at some times in my life more than others. It all had to do with making decisions through my deepest core values and leading myself more effectively.

Many of us are chasing the new car, the new house, the next vacation, or next thing that we think will bring us joy, happiness, and fulfillment. Then, we get it and wonder why we aren't happy. When we make decisions that are in line with our core values, we are not only happier and more fulfilled, but we are also more confident in our decisions that we will be making in the future.

One final story that will really hit this home. In the summer of 2021, my wife and I decided to invest in a backyard project for the home. We put in a massive patio. We completely remodeled the deck. We put in a huge firepit that overlooked a pond in our backyard. We even put in speakers and rigged a mount for a projector so we could watch movies as a family outside. We also did it because as our kids got older, we wanted our house to be "the house" that all of our kids' friends hung out at. We wanted their friends to come over and be with us instead of being elsewhere. We also wanted a space for our family to gather, have great conversations over a fire, and make memories. In July of 2021, the project was completed. It took seven months to complete, and it cost about 75K. I am not sharing the cost of the project to brag; it's relevant to the point I'll make below. We decided to have a big party with our kids and all of their friends. We must have had 20 kids and 15 couples over to break in the new space. We were playing cornhole and listening to music. We had food, drinks, soda, and snacks. At one point I sat back and just enjoyed watching everyone connect, smile, and enjoy themselves. My 16-year-old son came and sat with me. He put his arm around me and thanked me for letting him have all his friends over and told me what a great time he was having. Then the conversation went in a direction I didn't expect, but I am glad it did because it home a lesson for him and a powerful reminder for me.

He asked, "Dad, when are you going to by a nice car?"

I smiled and asked, "What are you talking about? My car is fine."

He said, "Dad, you have a 2016 Nissan Altima. It's a fine car. But when are you going to buy a really nice car?"

I asked "My car is fine buddy. I'm curious, why do you ask?"

He said, "Well, George (a neighbor and good friend of mine) just bought a brand-new Corvette Z06, Steve (another neighbor and good friend) just bought a brand new 'vette, and Jim (another neighbor and friend) has an Audi A8... Why don't you have a nice car, Dad?"

I smiled. I loved the question. I said, "Ethan, I don't value cars and I don't value stuff."

He looked puzzled and said, "I don't understand. Everyone likes new stuff and especially nice cars."

I put my arm around him and said, "Ethan, not everyone. Some people do, and that's OK. Some people even THINK they do and then find out they actually don't. I don't value nice cars. I value my family, making connections, making memories, and our environment/home. So, that's where I spend my money."

He looked puzzled and said, "I don't get it."

I continued, "Ethan, I don't value that stuff, man. I could have taken $75K and bought a really nice car, but that's not what I value. A nice car doesn't have much to do with connection with my family, making memories, or our environment. So, yes, I could have spent that money on a car, but it wouldn't bring me joy. If I am being really honest, you are sitting in my Corvette right now."

He looked totally confused. "What do you mean?"

I replied, "Ethan, this is backyard is my Corvette. I spend money that aligns with my values. Let me put it to you another way. I could have bought a Corvette and not spent money to do this backyard project. That might have been cool, but only you and I would be able to enjoy that while we were in it. Look around. Look at everyone here who is able to enjoy the money I spent on the backyard."

He looked up. He took a good look at all of his friends and everyone who was enjoying themselves. He took in the environment, the music, the food, laughter, and the memories that were being created right in front of him.

He looked back at me with a smile.

I asked, did I make the right decision, or should I have bought the car? The look in his eyes said it all. It clicked. I saw him come to life and have total clarity. He hugged me and said, "Good move, Dad!"

Guys, this is what I am talking about. Is there a part of me that is tempted to keep up with the Joneses and buy the next flashy car or thing? Sure. However, I run these decisions through my core values and really analyze if that decision is in line with my deepest core values and who I am as a man, husband, father, and leader. When we uncover our true core values, lead with them, and make decisions with them, life becomes more fulfilling.

If you don't know what your core values are, I highly encourage you to go through the Core Values Exercise at the end of this book. I have included the exercise so you too can find your core compass. What I can promise you is nothing more than a whole lot more clarity in your life. You may even feel like Neo when Morpheus gave him the red pill and he saw the Matrix for the first time. Neo was able to connect all the dots and fully realize how everything in his life had transpired.

Rule #9: Leverage Your Sense of Humor Every Chance You Get

Leading yourself, your wife, your kids, and even leading in the workplace will come with mistakes, learnings, and obstacles. How we handle those and respond accordingly is critical. Many men take their fatherhood journey very seriously, and we should. However, there is a balance where humor can play a key role in our enjoyment. Learning to laugh at ourselves or situations is a gift. I'm not saying all obstacles, mistakes, and learnings aren't sometimes tragic. A lot of them can be, and they will bring us to our knees and humble us. Every now and again, we can leverage our sense of humor and gift of being able to find the humor in any situation.

Effective leaders take their role seriously. However, that doesn't mean they take every single situation seriously. Great leaders are also FUN and find humor in situations and challenges. People (including our kids) are attracted to fun and positive energy. Leaders who take on every situation or challenge as a DO or DIE aren't the most pleasant to be around. Don't get me wrong. There is a time and a place for that mentality. However, we can't have that turned on 24/7/365. We will wear out the people around us and even ourselves.

Effective leaders not only lead people well, but they also create an environment and culture with a balance of fun and humor. Keep in mind your God-given gift of humor can be used to inspire. Don't forget that. Use it when you feel life is getting a little too serious.

Rule #10: You are the Spiritual Leader of Your Family

There are several things in life that will trigger an emotional reaction when we converse with others. It's always been a rule to not talk about politics, religion, sex, or finances in the workplace. If we look back at the past few years, since the COVID Pandemic began, we now have added COVID and vaccines to the list of things we should steer away from in conversation. All of the above topics can either bring us together on common ground or potentially tear us apart. In recent years, we have seen friends and families torn apart over disagreements about sensitive and politicized topics. It's been a stressful time of confusion, division, and uncertainty. Our spiritual journey is definitely at the top of the list when it comes to triggering others and being triggered ourselves. As we wrap up this book, let's have the conversation on faith and how it's either a part of your life or it's not. No matter your views on this topic or where you are on your own spiritual journey, I want you to know that you are respected. My views on this are simply that, my views. What I am about to share are simply my experiences.

Like I have mentioned throughout this book, I have heard thousands of stories from men over the years. The topic of their faith journey has come up numerous times. What I can tell you is that some men have had good experiences with faith growing up and some have had traumatic experiences. Some grew up being forced to believe a certain way, and if they didn't, they were shamed. I even know some men who were sexually assaulted by their pastors or other members of their church as children. On the other hand, some men grew up loving their faith and had fantastic experiences with family, church leaders, and church community. It was the one place they felt at peace in their lives, and it was important to them that their faith brought them together with others in their community.

Some men, like me, had experiences that were a bit of both. I grew up in a Catholic family, and there was a great deal of shame and guilt for sinning. I remember growing up that my grandmother would tell me I was going to hell if I missed mass on Sunday. When I was in fifth grade, I experience physical abuse from a priest.

I was a server when I was younger at our church. I really enjoyed it for many reasons, but there was one priest in particular who was extremely strict and quick to losing his temper. He was not only a priest at the church but also a teacher at the Catholic middle school that I attended. For some reason, he didn't really like me and he made it well known. I wasn't the best student growing up and always struggled with grades. The story that I tell myself is I probably didn't meet his expectations and I frustrated him. The day the abuse took place was a Wednesday morning towards the end of my fifth-grade year. I remember it vividly because it was a mass for the entire school (kindergarten – eighth grade). The priest and I were getting everything ready for the service. He was being his normal cold and distant self towards me and had zero patience for me that morning. He gave me tasks to do and made it very clear that he was in charge. He asked me to go get more matches for the candles on the altar, which were located in a room behind it. There were two rooms behind the church altar that stored everything needed for the services. I went back to the room where I thought the matches were stored. At the same time, everyone from my class was making their way to the church. They all had to pass by those two rooms.

Suddenly, I felt an arm wrap around my neck and put me in a choke hold from behind. At first, as I was being drug from behind into the other room, I thought it was an older student messing with me. After a few seconds, I realized that this wasn't a joke and it was perhaps someone bigger than an upper classman. In the other room, I was then pinned up against the wall by his hand on my neck. At that point, I was able to see who this person was—the priest. He got nose to nose with me as he held me by my neck and screamed at me. He told me I wasn't going into the right room and that the matches were in the other room. He scolded me for not listening. I was terrified as I saw the anger in his eyes and the intensity of his voice. As he released me, I looked outside the doorway of the room to see my entire class watch the whole thing as they walked by. Some of the kids in my class were shocked while others laughed at what happened. I was mortified. I was also terrified of this priest. I broke. I lost it. I began to cry and make my way to the other room. As I made my way to the other room, I heard the priest say, "Stop crying or I will give you something to cry about!" I served that mass with him that morning, and that was the last time I served mass ever again. After the service, I informed him I was quitting and wouldn't be back. He responded with, "Is that what you do in life when things get hard? You quit?"

I responded with, "I don't quit, but I won't be abused by you." I don't think he expected me to respond in such a way, and perhaps my response shed some light on the fact he had taken his discipline with me too far. Back then, it wasn't uncommon in my school for a teacher or priest to put their hands on a student out of anger. Back then, it was more accepted. However, it was still wrong. I quit that day and never really spoke of it until now. That experience and my upbringing made me question everything about my faith.

Into my adulthood, my faith was always in the background. It was like a smoldering flame that was barely illuminating. I would attend service on Easter and Christmas every year. I thought that was enough. Jessica and I got married in the Catholic faith, but at the time, I thought that was more for her than me. Jess grew up Catholic and she was very much in tune with her faith. She loved her faith and her relationship with God. Over the years, her faith has only gotten deeper. She has always prayed often and speaks confidently about her faith. When we were first married, without kids, she would always encourage me to attend mass with her on Sundays. Sometimes I would go and sometimes I wouldn't. At the time, I didn't see the need and wasn't really motivated. Going back to church would sometimes bring up negative memories from my childhood. I would even question my faith and at times wondered if there was a God because of my experiences with that priest. I knew deep down Jessica longed for a man to share in her faith and even lead her. There was a side of her that I know now felt empty, not having a man with his faith at the helm of his life.

When I became a dad for the first time in 2006, we had my son Ethan baptized in the Catholic faith. For me, at the time, it was a check of a box; something we had to do. Over the next several years, as the other three boys were born, Jessica and I would have the other three boys baptized as well. Our family continued to sporadically go to church over the next 14 years. We would attend here and there, but not often. It isn't easy to bring four noisy boys to church every Sunday! The story I would tell myself on Sundays is that the boys were too young to go. They would get bored and act out, which would disturb others around us. I justified that it was better we didn't attend. Plus, I wasn't in touch with my faith, and a big part of me felt very unworthy to be there. I felt like the biggest imposter being in church because I knew my heart wasn't in it. I attended church here and there because I knew it was important to Jess, but I wasn't leading my family. I was following and I was doing it poorly.

It wasn't until my oldest son, Ethan, was 14 years old that I started getting what I call "spiritual nudges" that I needed to deepen my faith. Ethan started getting curious about his faith. He really enjoyed mass on Sundays. He enjoyed praying and even praying out loud. He started asking me questions about the Bible, our beliefs, and even our traditions in the Catholic faith. Being honest here, I couldn't answer the majority of his questions. I couldn't give him reasons why we believed what we believed. I couldn't answer why we practiced the traditions we did. I simply responded to some of his questions with, "That's just what we do." Obviously, this response was a terrible way to lead. It also didn't give me any credibility with him. He would challenge me and ask, "Why don't you know? Why would we believe these things or do these things if you don't understand them?" He was right. I appreciate how he challenged me. At the time, however, it made me uncomfortable because he was in my face about the fact that I didn't have the knowledge about my own faith and I was just checking the box. I thought to myself, *What does my leadership look like for him? What does my example say to my son about faith, God, and our beliefs? How will this impact his personal faith journey growing up as he watches his dad simply check the boxes and continue on autopilot?*

Unfortunately, it wasn't this wakeup call that got me started on pursuing a deep relationship with God and keeping my faith at the helm of my life. The wakeup call actually came in 2019, and it was very unexpected. Back in 2015, I met a man, Brian McRae, at a local networking event that his organization was hosting. There were hundreds of business owners who attended, and the culture was all about generosity. There have been several networking events and organizations I have attended over the years. A lot of them were the same. Business owners would come together for self-serving reasons to promote their businesses for my clients. This event was very different. Everyone who showed up had the attitude of giving and helping each other. Every month Brian held these events where hundreds of us would get together to help each other. Brian was (and is) an amazing speaker with so much heart. Month after month, I saw him speak, inspire, and bring so many business owners together in the theme of GENEROSITY.

Brian and I became friends, but at first, it wasn't a close friendship—more of a distant, highly respected friendship. He was a huge fan of Dad Edge and everything I did. I was a huge fan of his and what he did at the local level. Brian has been married for 20-plus years with three grown daughters. I knew Brian was a man of faith, but at the time I didn't know how deep his faith ran. In 2016, Brian asked me to speak at one of his monthly events, which, at the time, was a huge deal for me. I had never spoken in front of 150 to 200 business owners on the subject of fatherhood. To me, this was the highest honor and compliment from someone I admired so much. I did the event. He enjoyed it, and so did the attendees. Over the next three years, Brian and I would become somewhat closer. We would meet for coffee every three months or so. I enjoyed our time together and respected him highly, as he was ten years older than me and ahead of me in knowledge. During our conversations, I would always lean into him for advice about life, business, marriage, and raising kids. He always had gems to share that were so helpful to a younger guy like me. He also answered my questions from a faith-informed perspective, but it was never over the top. I admired that about him. I thought it was amazing he had a deep relationship with God. We never really talked about the topic of faith specifically until 2019.

In 2019, Dad Edge really began to take off. *The Dad Edge Podcast* hit #1 Dad Podcast on iTunes for the first year and has continued to enjoy that same ranking for the past three. Our mastermind community (The Dad Edge Alliance) was growing quickly and became an incredible platform for so many husbands and fathers around the world. I began to think of ways to rattle the minds and hearts of men, husbands, and fathers. I saw the success our members were having in their marriages, parenting, mindset, and their health. We saw success stories on a daily basis! I wanted more men to achieve these same successes. I used social media to really help get the word out on what we were doing and how we were doing it.

I wasn't afraid to curse on the podcast or even in my posts. At the time, I thought that approach would help rattle the minds and hearts of men. I was wrong. One Wednesday morning, I got a text from Brian that read, "Hey man, how are you? Do you have time for coffee next week? I would really like to chat."

I didn't think there was anything alarming about the text and I replied with, "Absolutely! Let's do it!" We agreed upon a time and place for the following week. When I arrived at our usual coffee spot, I eagerly waited for Brian to arrive. I saw him walk in as I sat at our normal table. I stood to shake his hand and smiled. He shook my hand and looked me right in the eye with an expression I will never forget. He greeted me with happiness, but I could also sense some disappointment. I began to wonder why we were meeting and if I had done something wrong. The tension was so thick, I could cut it with a knife. We talked for about 30 minutes about family, work, and just life in general. I could tell he was gearing up to tell me something big and our coffee date was going to be more than just exchanging pleasantries.

"Larry, I invited you for coffee for a reason today," he began. I could tell even getting that first sentence out was tough for him. I could feel this conversation was heavy on his heart.

"Larry, I have seen some things on your social media and even in your podcast that concern me."

I took a deep breath because now I knew this was something big for him and I was going to get criticism about something I was doing. This wasn't easy because I looked up to Brian so much and valued his opinion.

"Larry, I have noticed a side to you that I really don't think is you. I have noticed you use language that perhaps isn't in line with your faith and who you are. Quite frankly, I don't think it's good for your brand or for your family."

I asked him to give me more detail and share some examples. He went on to tell me that I didn't hesitate to drop the F-bomb on podcasts or even in my posts. He went on to say, "Is that the branding you want? Is this in line with what you do and who you are? Do you think you can inspire men in a different way?"

I immediately got on the defensive because I felt a bit cornered into a conversation I didn't expect. I also felt like a kid who was in trouble with a parent who was disappointed in me. I began to defend it and state that it really wasn't a big deal.

Brian took a deep breath and began to ask me about my faith. "Larry, how is your relationship with God? What does your faith journey look like?"

At this point in the conversation, I felt extremely triggered. I didn't really want to have this conversation with anyone, let alone Brian. However, I set my ego aside because I wanted to hear more of what Brian had to say.

He went on to ask me again, "Larry, where are you at with your faith journey? What was your childhood like when it came to your beliefs?"

I took a deep breath and contemplated the question. The story I was telling myself before I spoke it aloud to Brian was that my faith walk felt like a maze at times. I felt like an imposter, and a part of me didn't even feel worthy to have a relationship with God. I was doing good work in the world and showing up for my family, but I had made so many mistakes in the past. There was such a strong part of me that felt unworthy of God's love. To be very honest, I had always been overwhelmed as to where to start. I didn't really understand the Bible, even after 12 years of Catholic education.

"Brian, I don't have the best relationship with God. I grew up Catholic, and to be honest my experiences growing up weren't the best. I am completely overwhelmed with the Bible and don't even know where to start. I have tried getting into it over the years and quite frankly, I don't understand a lot of it," I answered with shame in voice.

"Larry, I understand exactly where you are because a few years ago, I was there too. My faith walk was tough for me for years. My faith is solid now. I enjoy deepening my faith. I now identify as being the spiritual leader of my wife and three daughters. You have a tremendous positive platform and you are impacting millions of dads across the planet. You have such an opportunity to lead more men to their faith and lead your family as well," Brian explained.

Just hearing these words from Brian felt inspirational, but so far from my reach. I thought, *After all, who am I to inspire other men with their walk in faith? Currently, I don't have the best relationship with God and I am definitely not leading my family. I am leaning more on Jessica for our faith walk as a family.* The imposter syndrome was hitting me from all angles. However, I knew he was right. You might think that because I looked up to Brian, I would simply take in all he said and just accept it as truth. However, the more we talked, the more defensive I got.

"Brian, cursing isn't really that big of a deal. I can't promise you that I won't ever use language like that because I honestly don't think it's that important. Words are nothing more than the meaning we put behind them." Even though these words came out of my mouth, I knew they weren't me. Deep down I knew Brian was right. However, I didn't want to hear it. This was just another situation in my faith journey that was a negative experience.

"Larry, I get where you are at. However, I know you and I know your heart. This isn't the direction you want to go. You are raising four young men. Larry, I am raising three young women. My prayer is that Godly young men pursue my daughters' hearts. You not only have the opportunity to be the spiritual leader of your family but also inspire other men who you work with."

At this point in the conversation, I was still triggered. This was a subject that had brought me pain over the years. However, deep down, I knew he was right. The defensiveness I was feeling now was because of my own shame.

"Brian, thanks for the feedback. I'm sure this wasn't easy for you to tell me all of this," I said with a bit of shame and anger. We exchanged words for another few minutes before getting up to leave the coffee shop. We shook hands, but there was still tension. I wasn't happy hearing what he had to say and I could tell he felt awkward as well as we left.

I got in my car and sat in the parking lot. My blood began to boil a bit as I started going over the conversation in my head over and over. I started thinking about things he said about cursing on the podcast and on social media. I felt shame that someone like Brian, who I looked up to so much, would call me out on that. I felt even more shame and anger as I reflected on my own faith journey and how I neglected it. Plus, it was clear after the conversation that I was doing a really poor job leading my family. My anger began to build even more. There was even a side of me thinking, *Who does Brian think he is to tell me what I can and can't say?* However, I knew he was dead on. I knew he was right, which made me feel even worse. Over the next few days, I got even more angry recalling details of that conversation I didn't want to have and didn't even expect. I was angry and confused as to what I needed to do. Looking back on this situation now, I realize that what Brian did over coffee that morning was one of the most meaningful gifts of my life. That one conversation completely pivoted my entire life moving forward. I know now that it took so much courage and bravery for Brian to invite me to coffee and give me that tough love. He is a busy man and doesn't meet anyone for coffee often. So, the mere fact he took time out of his day and had a conversation with me that he was dreading as well says a lot.

After about three days, I picked up my phone to text Brian. As a I brought his name up on my phone, I knew that a text wasn't appropriate for a response to our face-to-face conversation. I was too ashamed to call him for fear it would turn into more tough love. So, I pulled up the voice recorder on my phone to record a voice message back to him.

"Brian, I know it's been a few days since our conversation and I have had some time to think about some of the things you said. After thinking about the conversation, I wanted to first thank you for taking the time to have the tough talk with me. I know it wasn't easy. At first, I wasn't happy with the tough love. To be honest, I was angry because it felt like another situation where I was questioned on my integrity with my faith. To add insult to injury, I felt you were also attacking Dad Edge. However, I have reflected on it, and you are 100 percent right with everything you said. To be honest, I haven't been the spiritual leader of my family. I don't even understand my faith myself. I don't know where to start."

After a few hours, Brian got back to me. He shot me a voice message back. "Larry, listen man, I love you, and there's nothing you can do about it. Good men watch out for other good men. You are a good man, and I got your back. I understand everything you are saying and I too have been there. Let me invite you to an event next week. It's a breakfast with an organization called CBMC (Christian Business Men's Connection). There will be breakfast with about 350 Christian businessmen from all over the local area. We have a Navy SEAL named Chad Williams who will be the speaker over breakfast. Chad wrote an incredible book called *The SEAL of Christ*. He will be speaking about his time in the SEALs and his faith journey. I would love for you to come."

When I heard about CBMC and Chad speaking, I was really intrigued. After all, I had interviewed over 25 Navy SEALs on the podcast and loved their messages. I had never heard of a SEAL speaking openly about his faith. I was in!

The following week, I showed up to that breakfast with Brian. There was about 350 Christian businessmen in the seats. Every single one of them was so nice to talk to. Every one of them were successful, and you could feel the humility and kindness in the room. It was so welcoming. I looked in the back of the room where I saw Chad behind a stack of his books, *The SEAL of Christ*. Brian introduced me to Chad, and we exchanged pleasantries. Chad didn't resemble the typical SEALs and special operators I had interviewed on the show. He was a shorter, stockier man in his late 30s with a big goofy smile on his face. He looked like just a normal dude, and his persona was one of fun and humor. Again, not your typical SEAL. He seemed confident, approachable, and fun.

The morning opened up with breakfast and a speaker before Chad. The speaker approached the podium and introduced himself as Eric. Just by the way he approached the podium, I could tell this man was about to share a powerful story. He owned a thriving business with over 50 employees. His business was worth millions. Back in 2017, his CPA noticed that they had made a huge mistake in paying payroll taxes, and the IRS had caught it. To make a long story short, the company owed nearly $500K in back taxes and penalties. Overnight, his business went from thriving to on a path to ruin. Over the next several months, things only got worse. The IRS froze his accounts (both personal and business). He was in jeopardy of losing his entire business and even his personal assets like his house. He was lost. He was overwhelmed and had no clue what to do.

He went on to share that a mentor of his from CBMC invited him to coffee one morning to hear more about what was going on. After Eric explained all the hardship, his mentor began to ask about his faith and where he was at with God. Eric was completely taken aback. *How could he even be asking about my faith and journey with Christ at a time like this?* Eric wondered. He was just trying to survive at this point. However, Eric listened. At this point, he wasn't going to turn anything down that could potentially help him.

His mentor invited him to go on a spiritual journey with him for the next two years. He invited him to a program called Operation Timothy. Operation Timothy (OT) is a relational discipleship tool named after the Apostle Paul's discipling of young Timothy. It is a progressive Bible study designed to help people grow spiritually and is rooted in the Great Commission, *"As you go, make disciples of all nations."* Put quite simply, Operation Timothy is a guided mentorship between a "Paul" (the mentor) to a "Timothy" (the student). This is a one-on-one mentorship where one man who has gone through and graduated OT can now mentor another through the process. The guided Bible study is conducted online and consists of three books with seven chapters in each. Each book has guided teachings, Bible verses, and reflection questions. The "Timothy" is meant to meet with his "Paul" every week or every other week for one to two years. The "Paul" guides his "Timothy" through the entire process. The goal is for the "Timothy" to deepen his faith and understanding of the Bible. It's also to help him become a mentor and a "Paul" for his future "Timothy." As overwhelmed as Eric was in his business, he accepted. Over the next two years he would dive into the online training and meet his mentor over coffee every week for 90 minutes.

He went on to explain that over the next two years, his faith became the helm of his life, his business, and family. His business restored back to profitability. He has now paid off the $500K in taxes and penalties. He kept his house, and everything is not only back to normal but better than it was. His family is now thriving in faith, and it was because he learned how to deepen his own faith and lead them. His testimonial was only about 10 minutes in length, but it was so powerful. At the time, I thought OT sounded like exactly what I was looking for, but I also felt I didn't have the time. After all, two years of study, online homework, and meeting with a mentor weekly sounded a bit daunting. After Eric spoke, he introduced Chad. Chad spoke for about an hour about his time in the SEALs and his journey with his faith. He was such a good speaker. He was lighthearted and funny, yet his stories were so powerful. I ended that morning with shaking Chad's hand and inviting him on the podcast, which he gladly accepted without hesitation.

The real magic came later that day when I checked my email. I saw I had an email from Brian, and the subject read, "Brian McRae has invited you to join Operation Timothy." I was taken aback big time by this. After all, OT seemed like a daunting project, and I didn't even think I was worthy for something like this. I also felt honored that Brian would invest in me like this. Going through OT and being someone's Paul is not a paid gig. It is 100-percent volunteer, and you do it out of love. Every part of me felt compelled to justify why I didn't have the bandwidth to do this. After all, I had a full-time organization to run with hundreds of members in our mastermind. I wanted to write another book (this one, funny enough). I had four boys to raise and all of their activities. I had a wife who needed my attention. At the time, my schedule couldn't really justify another project. However, despite all those feelings and justifications, I said YES. I looked up to Brian, and the fact he was willing to do this with me was such a compliment. We had our first meeting in January of 2020.

Over the next two years, we met every second and fourth Wednesday morning of the month from 7:00 a.m. to 8:30 a.m. I completed my online work between meetings and saw my faith deepen every single week. I began to understand the Bible and who Jesus was (and is). I began to understand God and the scriptures. When I didn't understand something, I had Brian right there to help me make sense of things. Meeting with Brian became a safe place and an opportunity to ask about anything that wasn't clear to me. I began going back to church on Sundays and inspiring my boys to want to go back to church. I began praying more often with Jessica, and we started having more conversations about our faith. I could tell these conversations were something that she had been longing for so long. She found joy, connection, and even elevated intimacy in our faith-based conversations. I also noticed that I was able to answer questions from my boys about scripture and the Bible, which gave me and them confidence in our beliefs. Over the next two years, not only did my faith and relationship with God deepen, but so did my entire family's. All of my boys actually look forward to church. They look forward to praying as a family and having open discussions. Looking back on those two years, I can tell you OT was exactly what I was looking for, and Brian was there guiding me the whole way.

If you ever think your kids don't watch your every move, I can tell you they do. Over that two-year time period, Ethan (14 when

I started OT and 16 now) began to ask me so many questions about OT. He thought the mentorship was amazing. When I was just about to graduate OT in 2022, Ethan asked me something I will never forget.

"Dad, when you graduate OT, you can become a Paul to someone else, right?"

I smiled and said, "Yes, I believe I can. However, I don't know if I am ready for something like that." The imposter syndrome was rearing its head once again.

"Dad, I would really like to go through that. Do you think you could be my Paul and take me through that?" he asked.

My thoughts raced through my head. I didn't think I was even close to doing anything like that for someone else. After all, I was just the student and learned so much of this in the past two years. It was all so new to me. Who was I to lead?

"Wow! Ethan, I am honored you would even ask me to do this. I'm speechless. My first response to this is absolutely! Let me think about what it could look like," I responded.

I simply gave him this answer to buy me some time to think on this and have a conversation with Brian. The next meeting I had with Brian I told him about Ethan's request. Brian smiled from ear to ear with love and gratitude.

"How did you respond, Larry?" he asked with a big proud smile.

"I told him I needed to think about what that would look like. I am being real here, Brian. I don't want to let him down. I still feel like the student here. What if I teach him the wrong things?" I shared.

Brian, still smiling and beginning to laugh, answered me, "Larry, this is the biggest compliment you could ever ask for. Your son is looking to you to lead him. I know you still feel like the student, but this is your next evolution in your faith journey. It's now time for you to lead, and by doing so, you will learn even more! I will be right there with you. If you get stumped, call on me for guidance and clarity. I got you. The answer to his request is YES!"

Hearing his words really hit me in the heart. After all, there truly is no greater compliment from a child than when he looks to his dad and asks him to teach him something. Not to mention, the request to deepen the faith of a teenager will not come very often. So, I seized it!

When Ethan came home from school later that day, I told him we were starting OT the next day. He beamed with joy! A huge smile from ear to ear accompanied a big hug from him. I knew it was the right thing to do. Even though I still felt like a beginner, I was in! I was in for the journey and the ride! I told him I may not know all the answers, but if we got stumped, we would have Brian to help us.

As I finish this book, I have been working with Ethan for the past several months every morning for 30 minutes. We get up early and meet before school starts. We start our mornings at 5:30 a.m. in the trenches of OT and scripture. We go through each reflection question and talk at length about each lesson. I have to tell you, it has not only done wonders for Ethan's faith; it has also created so much depth in our relationship as father and son. Teaching OT to Ethan has definitely become the next natural evolution in my own learning. I have learned that I don't have to be the master to teach something. I can still be the student that is just ahead of him, and by doing so, I learn more as well. Brian has been right there every time I have needed him. This experience over the past two years has been game changing and will be for the next year and a half with Ethan. I have committed to taking all four of my boys through this process.

I know this is a long story and perhaps one you didn't expect to read when you picked up this book. In fact, this story was one of the most difficult for me to share because there was a lot of confusion and even darkness around the topic. I share this story with you because I was in a place where I felt unworthy to have a relationship with God. I was so overwhelmed by the Bible growing up and even into adulthood. I didn't have a good relationship with God, even as an adult, and couldn't answer any of my kids' question relative to faith. I wasn't leading my family spiritually at all for years. I share this story with you because I now see how important this aspect of leading my family is. I always felt I led my family pretty well, but this was a major missing puzzle piece, and I was too overwhelmed to step into learning. I now realize how important this was (and is) to leading my family.

I share this story with you not to judge where you are in your faith journey. I share it because I struggled with it for so long. I still don't have all the answers, but I know more than I did. I am still a student of this journey and faith walk. I now start every morning in the Word with Ethan. We have a family group text where we share the Bible verse of the day and our reflections. We pray as a family often and enjoy church every Sunday. This walk has brought so much joy and humility to my life. Wherever you are with your faith journey, it's your journey. Perhaps your faith is like a five-alarm inferno and the foundation of how you live your life. Maybe your faith journey feels like mine did—overwhelming and accompanied by negative memories. Perhaps you are somewhere in between the two. Either way, I get it. This is not to say that this section is the be all and end all to inspire you to take action in your faith walk. However, maybe it will give you permission to start your faith walk as a student and to just be open to learning.

CONCLUSION

First and foremost, if you made it all the way here, I honor and appreciate you. I wrote this book from my heart to you. I know firsthand how the humbling journey of marriage, fatherhood, mindset, and even faith can impact so much of who we are. There is no manual for fatherhood. Society has set us up to simply "wing it and figure it out." By doing so, we go through it alone, blindly and frustrated. We view ourselves as weak and even imposters if we aren't executing flawlessly at all times. To add insult to injury, we don't ask for help or guidance from mentors or even peers. We perceive that if we ask for help we are weak. What we don't realize is that asking for help and speaking up inspires others who are quiet to do the same. I honestly believe with every part of my being that if we were able to open up the conversations with men more about our struggles in these areas, we would enjoy this journey so much more. When we change one man, we change a family. By changing a family, we change a community. By changing a community, we change a country. When we change a country, we change the world! Let's go impact the world in the pursuit of legendary fatherhood!

EXERCISE:
IDENTIFYING YOUR CORE VALUES

This exercise was reproduced with permission from Paul Gilbride Corporate Coaching for the purpose of helping you, the reader, identify your core values. Getting clear on what your core values are will enable you to become a better husband, father, and leader of your family.

To live a life in which we feel we are "being it all" we have to start with being honest and convicted about what is most important to us. What is non-negotiable in our lives? What are the virtues or values we strive to emulate that best define who we are at our core? Answering these questions provides the foundation on which we will build our "Being Statement"—the statement that will define our mission in life. It is an exercise that forces us to really contemplate what we stand for, what we are passionate about, and what gives our life meaning and purpose. This exercise, despite its critical importance, can be simple if you break it into the following steps.

Start with the list of core values. This is a very comprehensive list, but feel free to add your own if you feel strongly about something that is missing. From this list, you are going to identify your top five to seven core values.

Step 1

Go through the list line by line. Eliminate any value that you know for sure is either not important to you or not important enough that it would even come close to making your top five to seven. Cross out those values.

Step 2

Start at the top of the list of values that remain after step 1. Compare the first value on the list to the next value on the list and ask yourself this question: If I could only live one of these values, which one would it be? In other words, which one is more important to you? Once you choose between those two, compare the one you chose with the next value on the list and ask yourself the same question. Continue to take the most important value you choose and compare it to the next one on the list. When you get to the end of the list, the value that you selected in the last comparison is your most important value. Write it down on the Core Values and Being Statement Worksheet and cross it off the list of values.

Step 3

Repeat Step 2 with the remaining list of values until you come down to the last two again. The one that is the most important value of the last two is your second most important value. Write it down on the Core Values and Being Statement Worksheet and cross it off the list of values. Continue to repeat Step 2 until you have written down your top seven values.

Step 4

Lastly, take a real close look at the seven values you have selected. Ask yourself: Are the last two critical? Are they game changers? Do I have a similar passion for those last two that I do with the first five? If the answer to any of these questions is no, eliminate them from the list. Five is ideal, but six or seven can work as well. Just make sure they are critical for you to really live as your authentic self.

One very important thing to keep in mind while doing this exercise is to choose from a place of passion and purpose, not from fear. If you feel as though a value is important to you because you think you have to be that way, you are choosing it out of fear. If you are choosing it because you want to be that way, that is the power in choosing the values that will reveal your true nature.

The "Being Statement"

This is where you will articulate, in whatever form that works for you, what you stand for and how you live your life. It will be based on your five to seven values and it will become the mantra to which you will measure yourself every day.

Tense matters

It is important that this statement be written as though you already live this way. That it is who you are at your core. It is not how you are going to be; it is how you are. For example, if part of your "Being Statement" is, I will seek opportunity in everything that happens in my life, that should be rewritten to say, "I seek opportunity in everything that happens in my life." Forget the word "will." There is an amazing power to reading your "Being Statement" in a manner in which you are already there, living and breathing it. You can be those values now. Those values are you, and so it should be expressed that way.

Keep it simple
The most effective "Being Statements" are generally three to five sentences long. You might even want to consider a bullet-point approach if that is more effective for you.

Share it
When you are done, share it with people you know and trust. This makes it real…and they may even have some valuable feedback for you.

Keep it relevant
Your "Being Statement" is your declaration to you and the world of who you are and what you stand for. Laminate it and put it in your purse or wallet. Make it your screen saver. Tape it on your bathroom mirror. Whatever it takes to be constantly reminded of what makes you most you…please do it! It will begin to permeate through all your thoughts and actions. Eventually who you are and how you show up in the world will be one. That is power! That is having it all!

Use the Core Values and Being Statement Worksheet to draft your "Being Statement." The section before the worksheet consists of examples to help you craft your "Being Statement" in a way that is most meaningful for you.

List of Core Values

Accomplishment	Creativity	Gratitude
Accountability	Curiosity	Grounded
Accuracy	Determination	Growth
Acknowledgement	Dignity	Happiness
Adaptability	Directness	Harmony
Adventure	Discovery	Health
Altruism	Diversity	Helpfulness
Ambition	Ease	Honesty
Authenticity	Efficiency	Home
Balance	Effortlessness	Honor
Beauty	Empowerment	Hope
Being the Best	Equality	Humility
Belonging	Enthusiasm	Humor
Boldness	Environment	Idealism
Calm	Ethics	Inclusion
Caring	Excellence	Initiative
Career Achievement	Fairness	Independence
Challenge	Family	Innovation
Collaboration	Financial Stability	Integrity
Commitment	Flexibility	Intuition
Community	Focus	Job Security
Competence	Forgiveness	Joy
Compassion	Freedom	Justice
Comradeship	Friendship	Kindness
Confidence	Fun	Knowledge
Connectedness	Future Generations	Leadership
Contentment	Generosity	Learning
Contribution	Gentleness	Legacy
Cooperation	Giving Back	Leisure
Courage	Grace	Listening

Love	Recognition	Success
Loyalty	Reliability	Tact
Making a Difference	Respect	Teamwork
Nature	Responsibility	Thrift
Openness	Resourcefulness	Time
Optimism	Risk Taking	Tolerance
Order	Romance	Tradition
Orderliness	Safety	Travel
Parenting	Security	Trust
Participation	Self-Esteem	Truth
Partnership	Self-Expression	Uniqueness
Passion	Self-Discipline	Usefulness
Patience	Self-Respect	Understanding
Patriotism	Serenity	Unity
Peace	Service	Vision
Personal Fulfillment	Simplicity	Vitality
Presence	Spirituality	Vulnerability
Perseverance	Spontaneity	Wealth
Power	Sportsmanship	Well-being
Pride	Stewardship	Wholeheartedness
Productivity	Strength	Wisdom

"Being Statement" Examples

Example 1

Core Values – Compassion, Optimism, Confidence, Integrity, Patience

Being Statement – "I live with confidence in who I am and the gifts I have to share. I always see the best in everything and everyone and have compassion for myself and all those I meet. I am true to my word and practice patience in letting my life unfold in its own way."

Example 2

Core Values – Curiosity, Innovation, Spontaneity, Tolerance, Generosity

Being Statement – "I view all things in my life with curiosity rather than judgment. I give to the world through my constant quest to be innovative and look for a better way. I am tolerant of everyone I meet, as we all have our own story and journey we are on. I give of myself every day and follow my intuition to lead me in all moments."

Example 3

Core Values – Helpfulness, Service, Fun, Honesty, Wisdom

Being Statement – "I seek constant growth in myself to create wisdom and perspective. I share all that I have learned with others as a way of giving back to the world and serving a higher power. I seek fun in everything I do. I practice integrity and honesty with myself and everyone I meet."

Your Core Values and Being Statement Worksheet

Top 5 – 7 Core Values:

1. _____
2. _____
3. _____
4. _____
5. _____
6. _____
7. _____

"Being Statement"

_____
_____
_____
_____
_____
_____
_____
_____
_____
_____
_____
_____
_____
_____
_____
_____
_____
_____
_____

LETTER TO MASON

The Summit of Mt. Quandary – 14,265ft
Rite of passage from being a boy to a young man...

Dear Mason:
I wanted to take you on this trip for so many reasons. This summit to the top of Mt. Quandary represents the end stages of you being a boy and the beginning stages of you being a man. It's called a rite of passage. Rites of passage have been around for centuries. A rite of passage is when you experience something that takes work and is then celebrated after completion. As you sit on this mountain and read this letter, you are no longer a little boy. You have reached the peak (just like you did on this mountain) of boyhood...now you will start the journey of being a young man.

Being a young man means so many things. It means you will now have more responsibility. Your choices (good and not so good) will have bigger and more profound outcomes. It's time to really start understanding things like: relationships, friends, trust, how you treat girls, money, working hard in school, working hard in life, working hard in sports, never giving up, doing hard things, taking care of your body, taking care of your mind, doing things that will make you stronger, wiser, and better every day.

Trust/Honesty: Now that you are becoming a young man, trust and honesty is something that is critical. Always tell the truth. You will not get in trouble with us when you are honest. You won't be punished for being honest, even if you made a bad decision.

Honesty and trust is the foundation of any relationship. If people can't trust you, you won't have the freedom to enjoy the things that you want out of life.

Always stand up for what you believe in: As you get older, you will have dreams and aspirations to do great things. People around you (even friends) will always try and pressure you to do things that aren't the wisest choices. Your friends, at some point, will tempt you with drugs, alcohol, stealing, or even bullying someone who is weaker. I already know your beliefs on all of this and I know it's not what you believe in. People who you think are your friends and have your back will tempt you to do all the above and more. Always stand your ground...stand up for what you believe in...no matter what people say and do.

Women in your life: As you get older, you will start dating. You will be dating a variety of women in your life that will all have different personalities. You will fall in love...probably several times in your life. Always treat women with the utmost respect. Open doors for them. Use manners. Never force them to do anything physical (like sex or kissing) if they aren't ready. Always treat a woman's parents with the utmost respect. Keep in mind you are dating their daughter... so they need to trust you. On another note, never let a woman take advantage of you. There are some women in the world that don't treat men well. They are disrespectful...they can call you names... they can even mess around on you with one of your friends. Never stand for that. I've dated women like that, and they will suck the life out of you. There are women in the world that will treat you with so much love and kindness (much like Mom treats me). My hope is that you see how Mom and I treat each other. I fully know that we aren't perfect parents (no parents are). Every parent out there has their strengths and weaknesses. But there is one thing that is a huge strength for me and your mom...that is our love and respect for each other. I can tell you without a doubt that 9 out of 10 marriages are not like mine and Mom's. Most marriages are a disaster in some way. This is one cool thing you get to witness as you grow up...a healthy relationship between a man and a woman. I never had this growing up...except for my grandpa. Mom and I don't call each other names. We hug. We kiss. There isn't a day that goes by that we don't tell each other how much we love and appreciate each other. We are good friends. We are good teammates. We have each other's backs no matter what. As you get older, my hope is that you find the same relationship with a woman or even better.

Managing money: As you get older, managing money will be extremely important. Most adults have ZERO skills when it comes to managing money. For the most part, a lot of people are broke. I know you see that a lot of people have nice cars, nice houses, and a lot of STUFF. What you don't see is most people struggle with money because they are spending money on all that stuff and saving ZERO of it. Most people become slaves to their jobs and slaves to money because they have no idea how to manage it or how to use it as a powerful tool. My promise to you is to teach you all of that. You just have to promise to be a good student. If we do it right, you won't have to work for anyone when you get older. You can start your own business. You'll have enough money that you won't have to worry and you can do work that truly makes you come alive. Bottom line is this...you manage money...it doesn't manage you. Always save at least 20 – 30 percent of what you make (in other words, save at least $3 for every $10 you make). When you save like that, you are buying years of financial freedom down the road. Also, don't spend money you don't have. I know you see me and mom spend a lot of money on a credit card...however, we never spend more money than what we have. Credit cards don't mean you can spend money without tracking it; it means you pay the credit card balance off every month. If you don't have the money to pay for something...go make the money you need to pay for what you want. I will teach you all this stuff.

Friendships: You will have a variety of friends in your life as you get older. You will have some friends that are super close. You will have others that you talk to often, but you might not feel a deep connection to them. Believe it or not, most friends will come and go. The secret to good friends is finding friends who have your back, your best interests, and the ones who always want what is best for you. You even will want friends that will call you out on your bullshit. LOL! I know that doesn't make much sense now, but trust me it will later. You want friends (young men) in your life that have the IRON SHARPENS IRON mentality. Again, I know this might not make much sense now...but as you get older, I will continue to explain this to you. IRON SHARPENS IRON means you have men in your life that always want what is best for you, even when you can't see it. I know you have seen me with friendships in my life that don't really serve me. On the other hand, you seen other men in my life would come to me in my darkest times. We support each other through anything and everything. That is what you will want to find as you get older as well.

Leadership: I can tell already that you have the potential to be a great leader. A great leader is someone who is strong, confident, and HUMBLE. A leader helps others develop and they are always looking to serve others. They help pick others up. They step when things get hard and difficult.

Do things right the first time: You already know this, but there are two ways to do anything in life. 1. Take shortcuts and do things wrong. 2. Do things right the first time. The first option will ALWAYS be a temptation because at the end of the day...it's easy. The second option will usually be harder but will always be rewarded. For example, it's fast and easy not to brush your teeth... but over time, your breath will start to stink, your teeth will rot, and your mouth will be disgusting. Another example is it can be easy to not study for a test because it takes time and work. But not studying usually results into a pretty poor grade. Poor grades usually result in not going to the school you want to or the job/business you want to have later. It's easy to watch TV and not clean your room. But if your room is a total mess and we have a fire in the house, the firefighters are going to have a tough time getting to you if they are tripping on your stuff. Take care of your gear...and your gear will take care of you.

Mason, it's truly an honor being your dad. I know sometimes I can be tough on you and you probably hate me for it. But in the end, I'm here to guide you, to teach you, and to help you grow into a man. You already are an amazing young man with so many incredible qualities. Raising you has been and always will be an honor.

I love you more than anything. I am proud of you for so many reasons. I am proud to have done this trip and climbed this mountain together. It has been an awesome experience.

Love you,
Dad

www.ingramcontent.com/pod-product-compliance
Lightning Source LLC
Chambersburg PA
CBHW062153080426
42734CB00010B/1674